Wight Sr

· I.O.W CAR

by

Besley

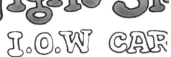

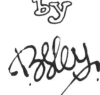

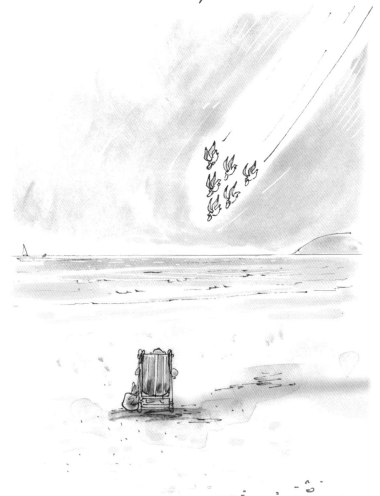

Eight years have passed since the appearance of Wight Smiles 3, the last such collection of local cartoons. Time for another round-up.

150 of the cartoons in this selection first appeared in the Isle of Wight County Press between 2007-2015. Around 25 others, not previously published, have been added in for good measure.

Acknowledgements -

Thanks as ever to all at Crossprint and the County Press and, for this publication, particular thanks to Robin Freeman, Managing Director of the CP, and to Barry Smith, Designer at Crossprint.

BEFORE THEY BUILT THE LIGHTHOUSE ...

CONTENTS

CAN YO' HEAR ME, NEWPORT... COWES... RYDE... SANDOWN... VENTNOR...TOTLAND... PORTSMOUTH ...

That Stretch of Water

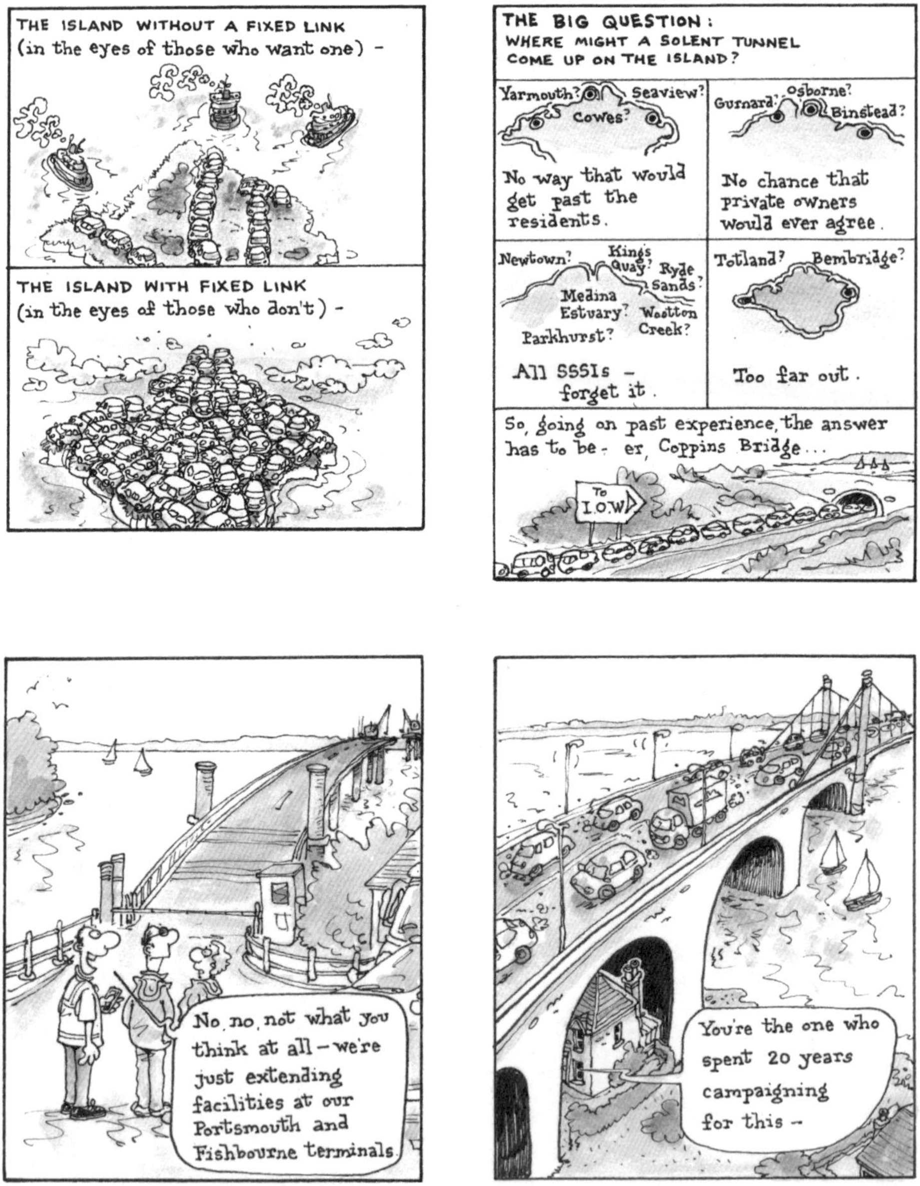
THE ISLAND WITHOUT A FIXED LINK
(in the eyes of those who want one) -
THE ISLAND WITH FIXED LINK
(in the eyes of those who don't) -
THE BIG QUESTION:
WHERE MIGHT A SOLENT TUNNEL COME UP ON THE ISLAND?
Yarmouth? Seaview? Cowes?
No way that would get past the residents.
Gurnard? Osborne? Binstead?
No chance that private owners would ever agree.
Newtown? King's Quay? Ryde Sands? Medina Estuary? Wootton Creek? Parkhurst?
All SSSIs - forget it.
Totland? Bembridge?
Too far out.
So, going on past experience, the answer has to be - er, Coppins Bridge...
To I.O.W.
No, no, not what you think at all - we're just extending facilities at our Portsmouth and Fishbourne terminals.
You're the one who spent 20 years campaigning for this -

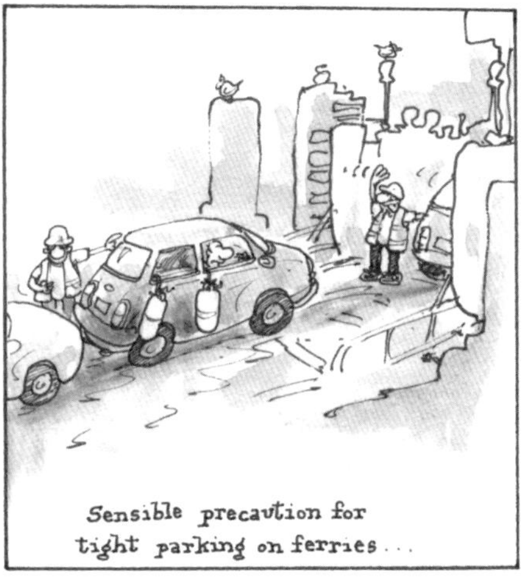

Sensible precaution for tight parking on ferries...

HEART-SINK MOMENTS ON THE I.O.W (No. 39):

You've just found yourself a nice quiet seat on the ferry, when...

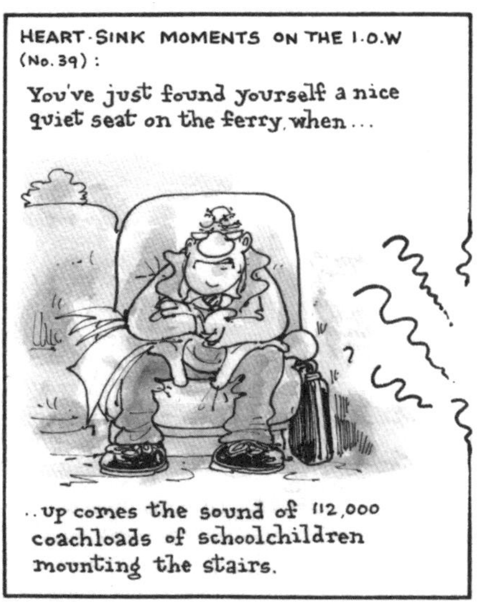

..up comes the sound of 112,000 coachloads of schoolchildren mounting the stairs.

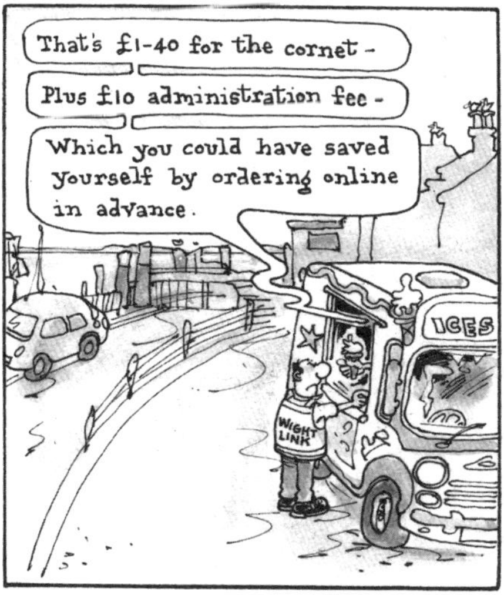

That's £1-40 for the cornet -
Plus £10 administration fee -
Which you could have saved yourself by ordering online in advance.
ICES
WIGHT LINK

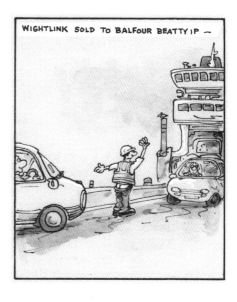

WIGHTLINK SOLD TO BALFOUR BEATTY IP –

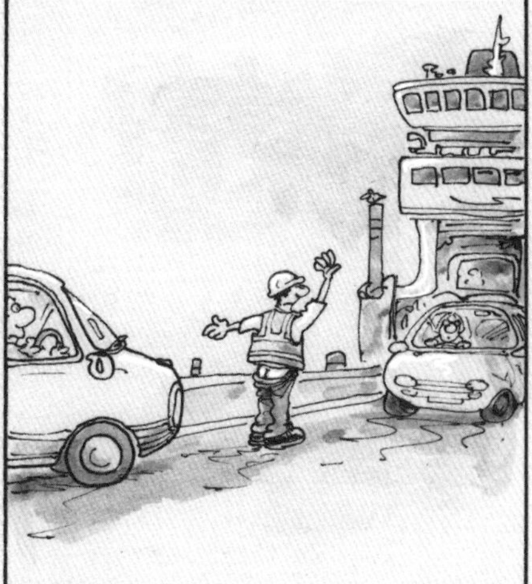

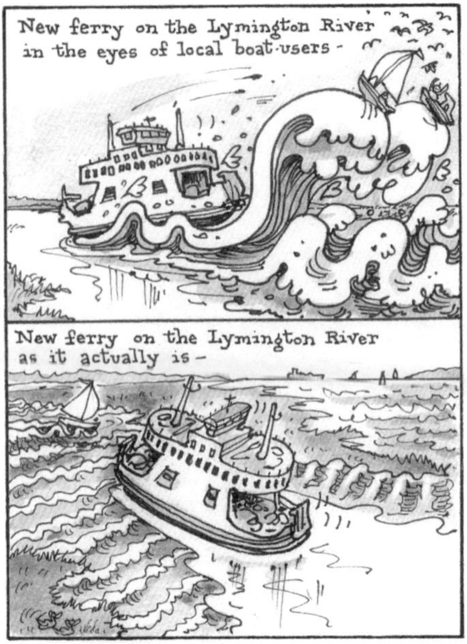
New ferry on the Lymington River in the eyes of local boat-users -
New ferry on the Lymington River as it actually is -

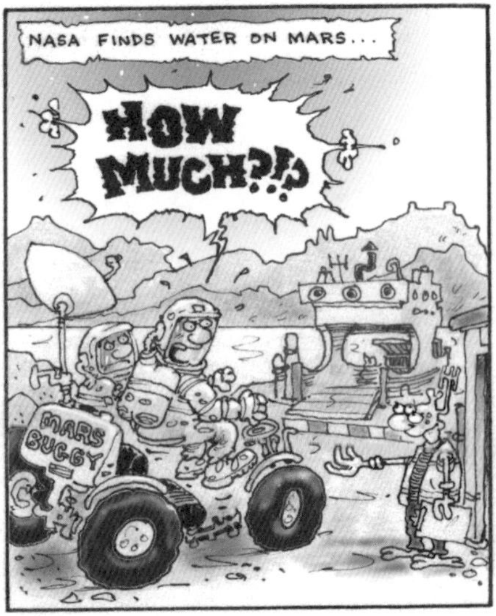
NASA FINDS WATER ON MARS...
HOW MUCH?!?
MARS BUGGY

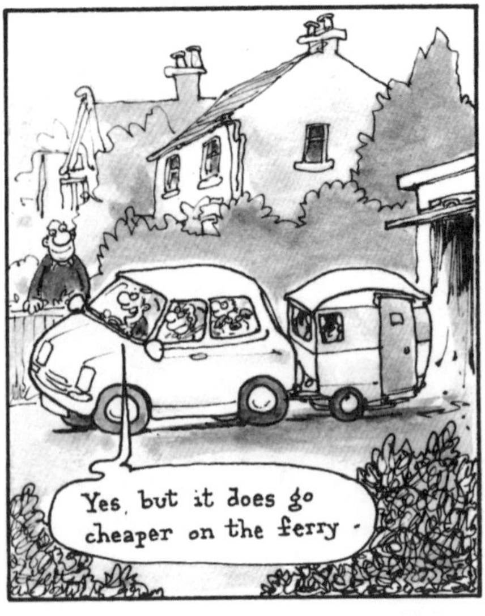
Yes, but it does go cheaper on the ferry -

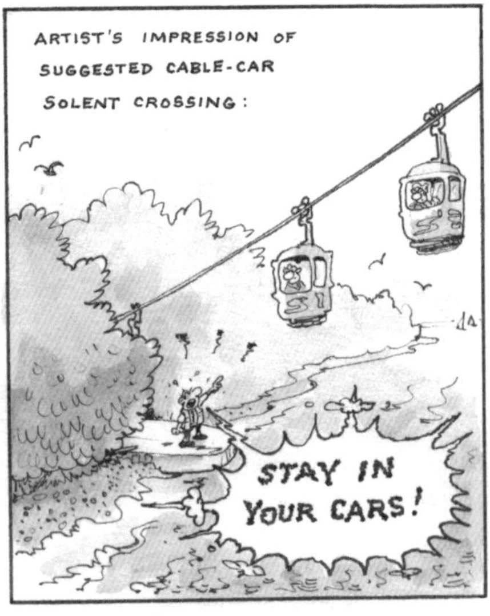
ARTIST'S IMPRESSION OF SUGGESTED CABLE-CAR SOLENT CROSSING:
STAY IN YOUR CARS!

Over Here, Round the Island

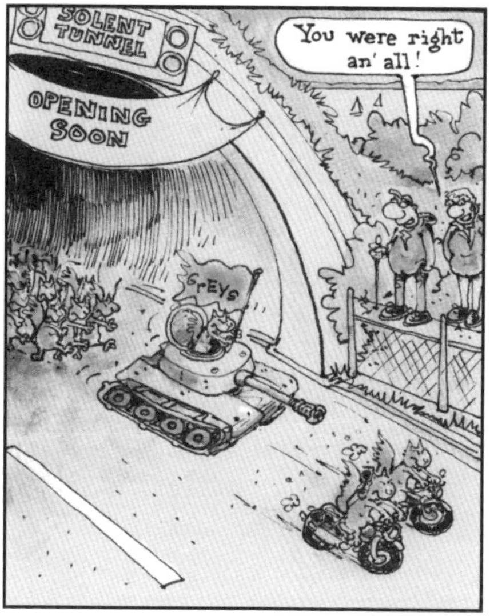
SOLENT TUNNEL
OPENING SOON
GrEYS
You were right an' all!

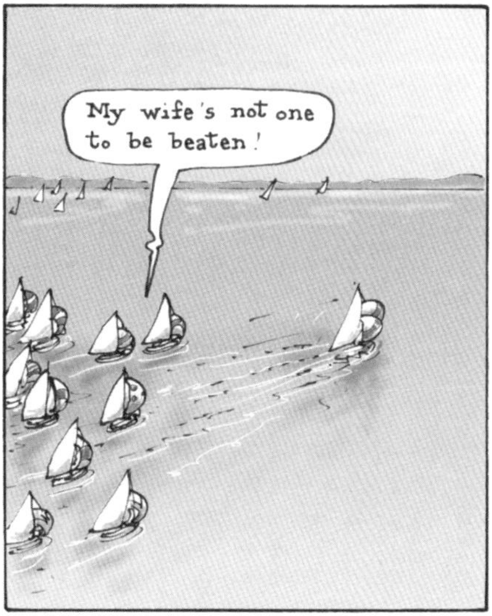
My wife's not one to be beaten!

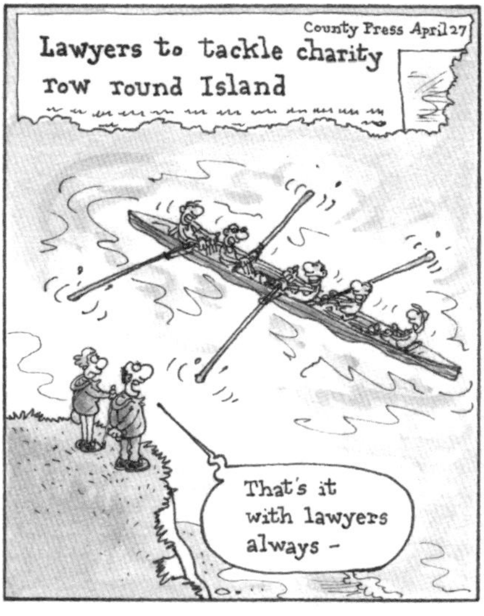
County Press April 27
Lawyers to tackle charity row round Island
That's it with lawyers always -

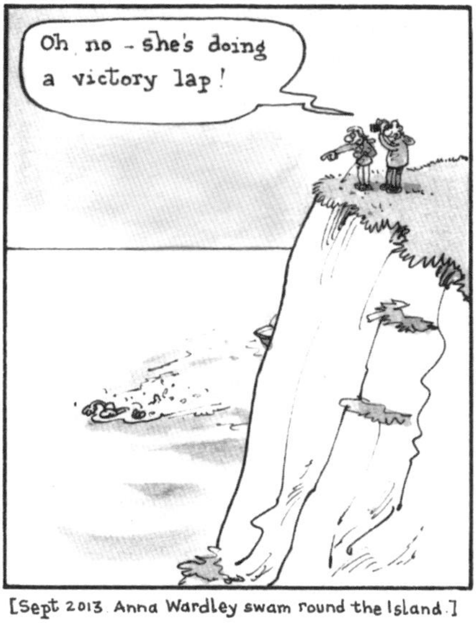
Oh no - she's doing a victory lap!

[Sept 2013. Anna Wardley swam round the Island.]

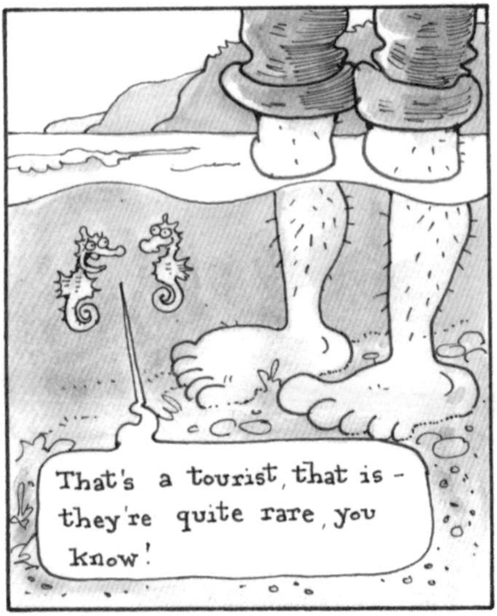
That's a tourist, that is - they're quite rare, you know!

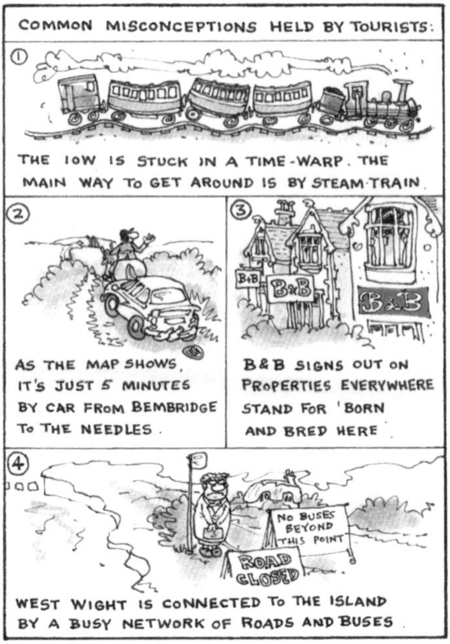
COMMON MISCONCEPTIONS HELD BY TOURISTS:
1
THE IOW IS STUCK IN A TIME-WARP. THE MAIN WAY TO GET AROUND IS BY STEAM-TRAIN.
2
AS THE MAP SHOWS, IT'S JUST 5 MINUTES BY CAR FROM BEMBRIDGE TO THE NEEDLES.
3
B&B
B&B
B&B
B&B SIGNS OUT ON PROPERTIES EVERYWHERE STAND FOR 'BORN AND BRED HERE'.
4
NO BUSES BEYOND THIS POINT
ROAD CLOSED
WEST WIGHT IS CONNECTED TO THE ISLAND BY A BUSY NETWORK OF ROADS AND BUSES.

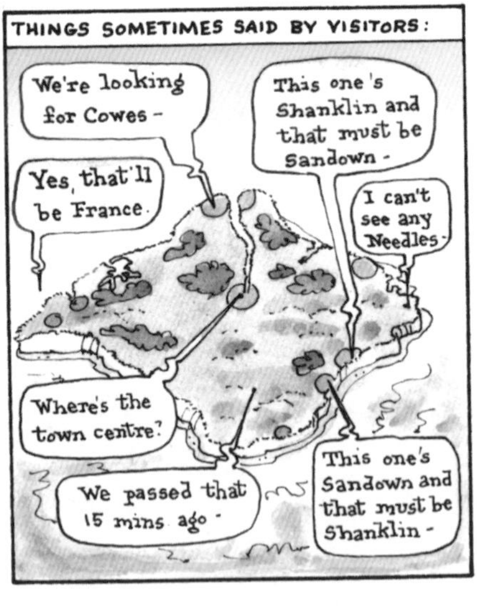
THINGS SOMETIMES SAID BY VISITORS:
We're looking for Cowes -
This one's Shanklin and that must be Sandown -
Yes, that'll be France.
I can't see any Needles -
Where's the town centre?
We passed that 15 mins ago -
This one's Sandown and that must be Shanklin -

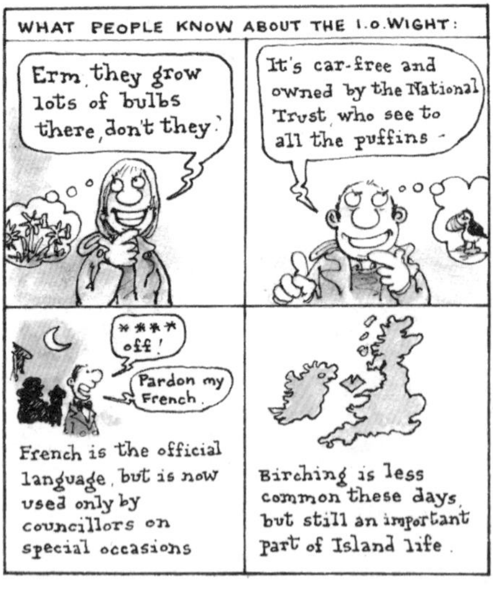
WHAT PEOPLE KNOW ABOUT THE I.O.WIGHT:
Erm, they grow lots of bulbs there, don't they?
It's car-free and owned by the National Trust, who see to all the puffins -
**** off!
Pardon my French.
French is the official language, but is now used only by councillors on special occasions
Birching is less common these days, but still an important part of Island life.

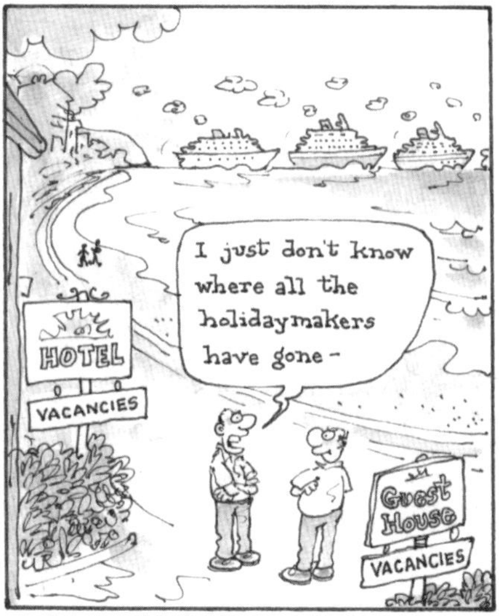
HOTEL
VACANCIES
I just don't know where all the holidaymakers have gone -
Guest House
VACANCIES

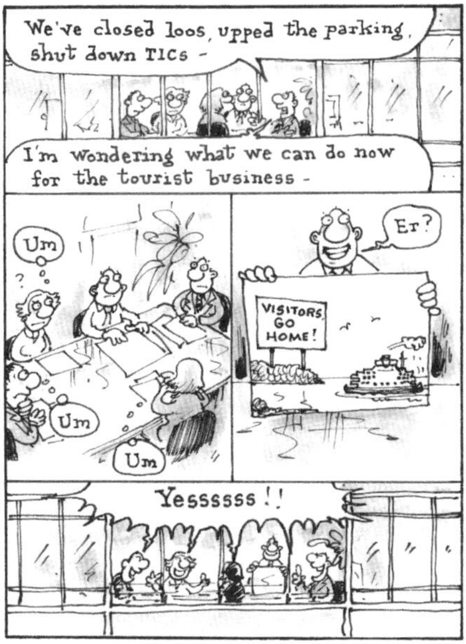
We've closed loos, upped the parking, shut down TICs -
I'm wondering what we can do now for the tourist business -
Um
Um
Um
Er?
VISITORS GO HOME!
Yesssss!!

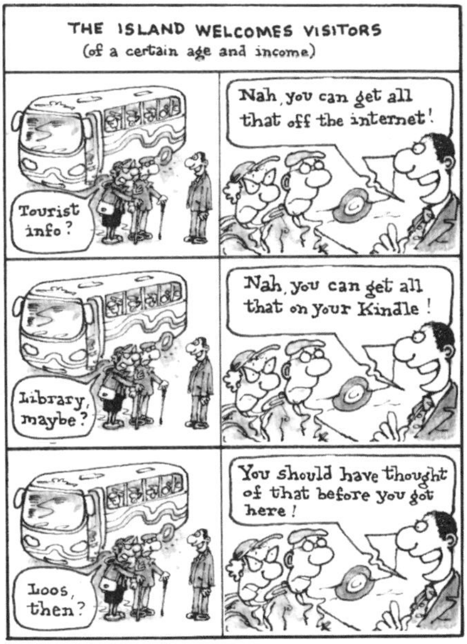
THE ISLAND WELCOMES VISITORS
(of a certain age and income)
Tourist info?
Nah, you can get all that off the internet!
Library, maybe?
Nah, you can get all that on your Kindle!
Loos, then?
You should have thought of that before you got here!

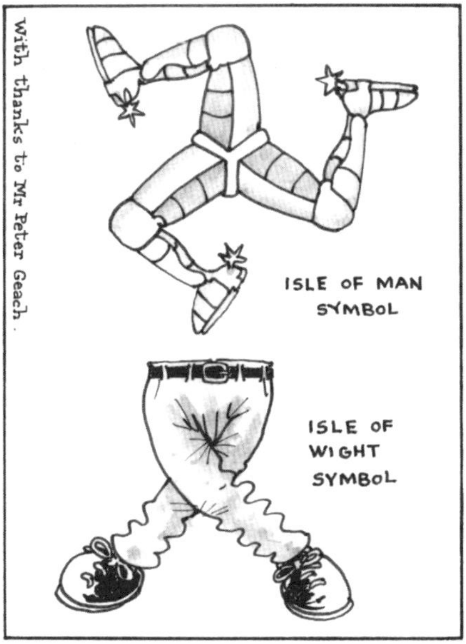
With thanks to Mr Peter Geach.
ISLE OF MAN SYMBOL
ISLE OF WIGHT SYMBOL

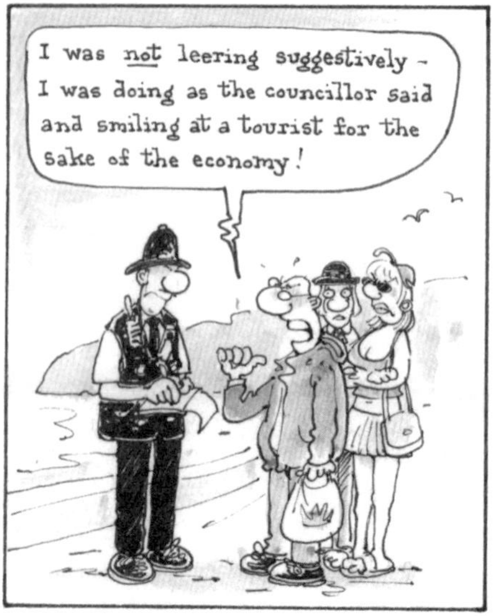
I was not leering suggestively - I was doing as the councillor said and smiling at a tourist for the sake of the economy!

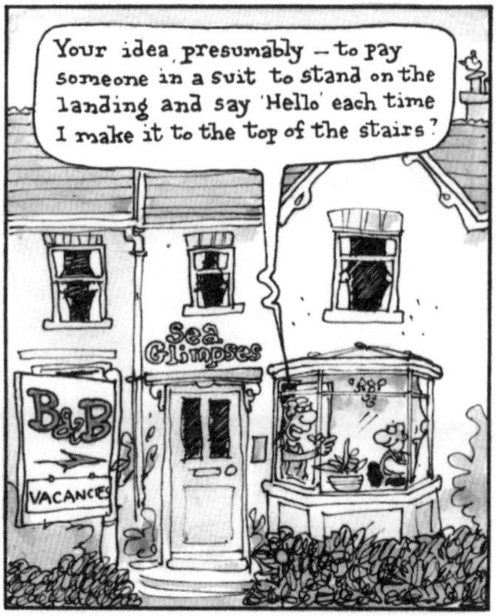
Your idea, presumably - to pay someone in a suit to stand on the landing and say 'Hello' each time I make it to the top of the stairs?
Sea Glimpses
B&B
VACANCES

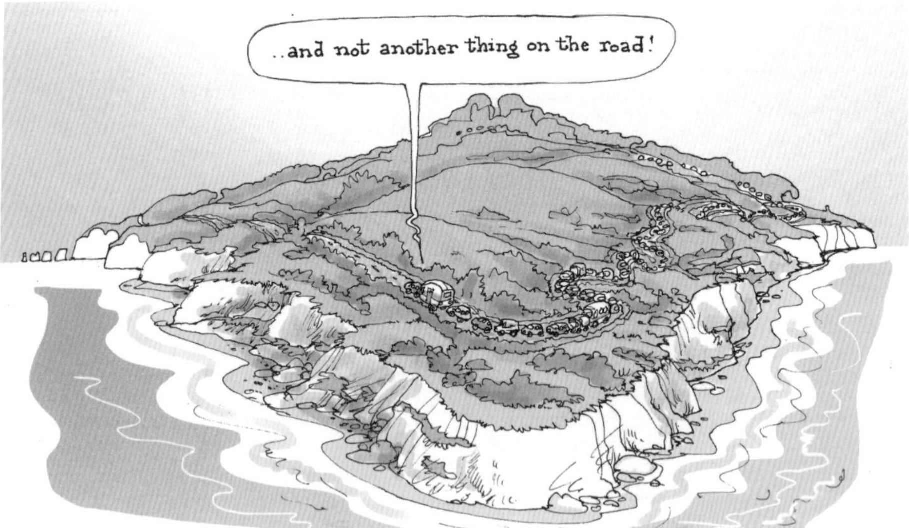
..and not another thing on the road!

Festive Mode

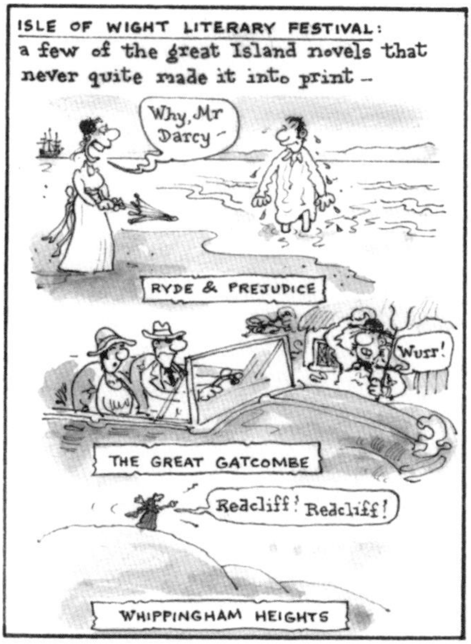
ISLE OF WIGHT LITERARY FESTIVAL:
a few of the great Island novels that never quite made it into print -
Why, Mr Darcy -
RYDE & PREJUDICE
Wurr!
THE GREAT GATCOMBE
Redcliff! Redcliff!
WHIPPINGHAM HEIGHTS

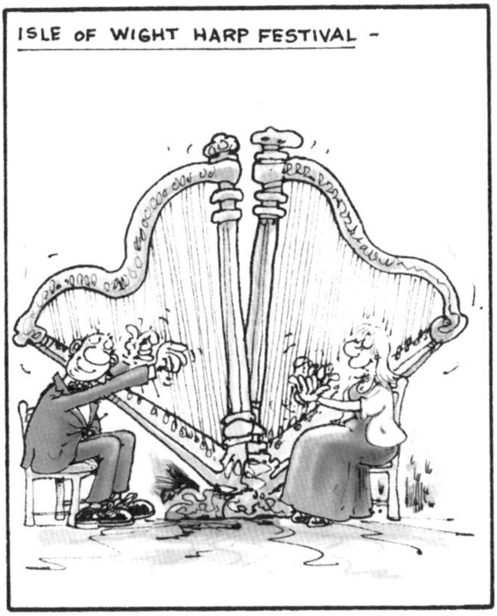
ISLE OF WIGHT HARP FESTIVAL -

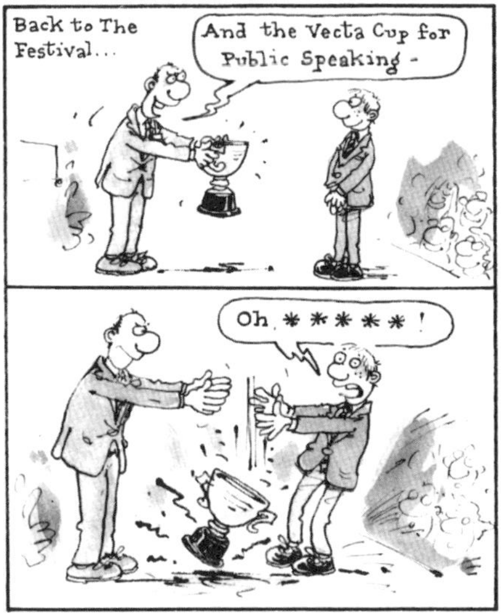
Back to The Festival...
And the Vecta Cup for Public Speaking -
Oh *****!

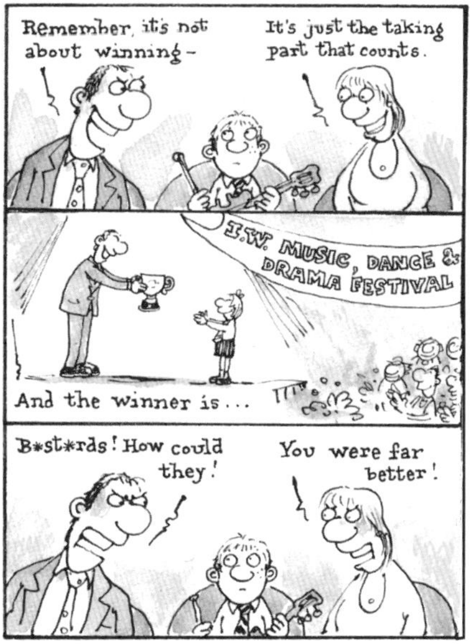
Remember, it's not about winning -
It's just the taking part that counts.
I.W. MUSIC, DANCE & DRAMA FESTIVAL
And the winner is...
B*st*rds! How could they!
You were far better!

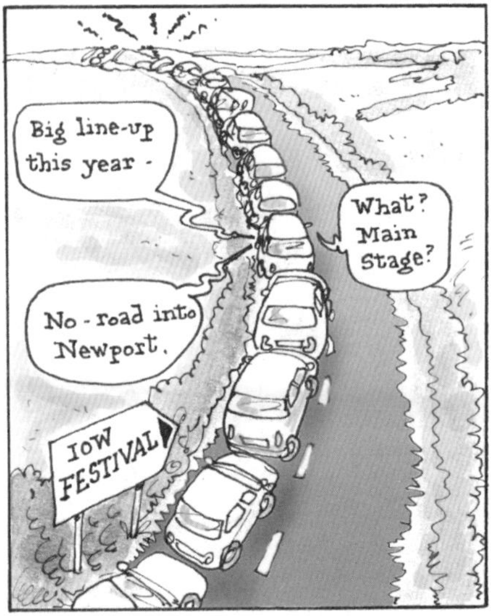
Big line-up this year -
What? Main Stage?
No - road into Newport.
IOW FESTIVAL

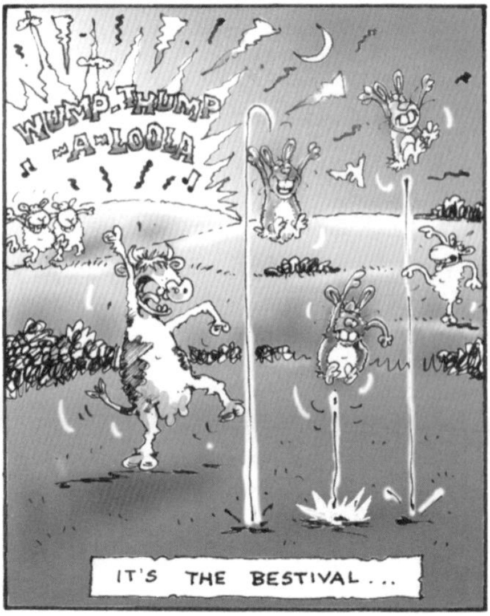
WUMP-THUMP -A-LOOLA
IT'S THE BESTIVAL ...

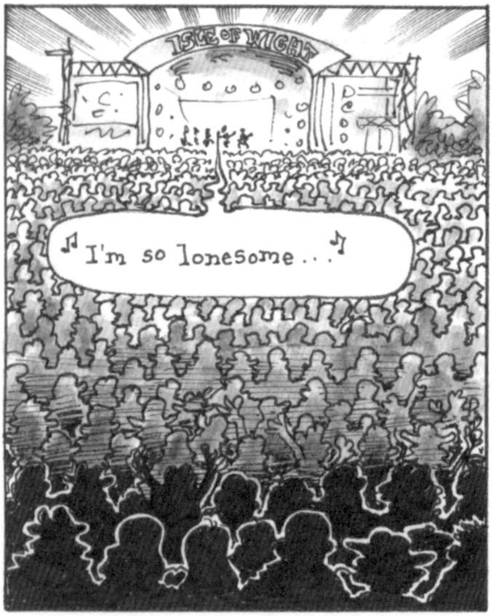
ISLE OF WIGHT
I'm so lonesome ...

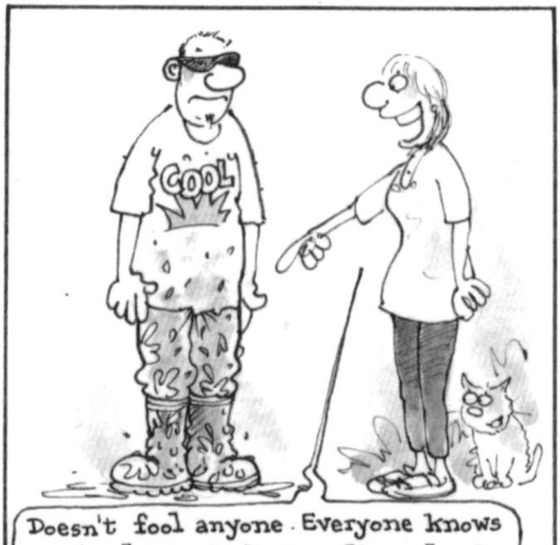
COOL
Doesn't fool anyone. Everyone knows you've been gardening all weekend, not boogeying at the Bestival!

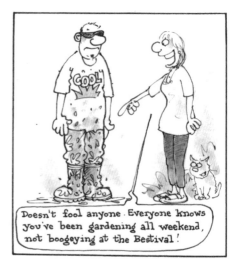

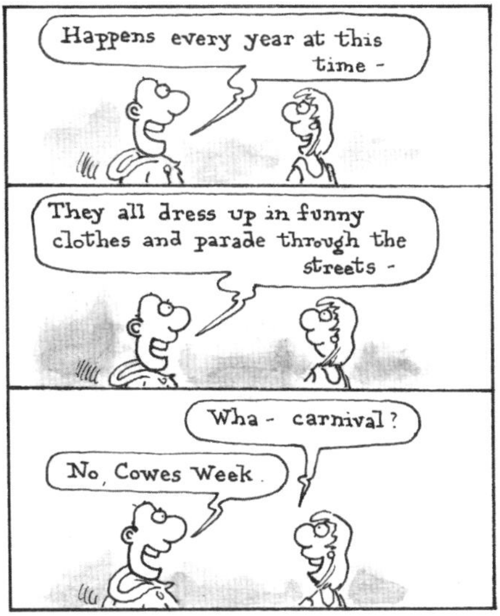
Happens every year at this time -
They all dress up in funny clothes and parade through the streets -
Wha - carnival?
No, Cowes Week.

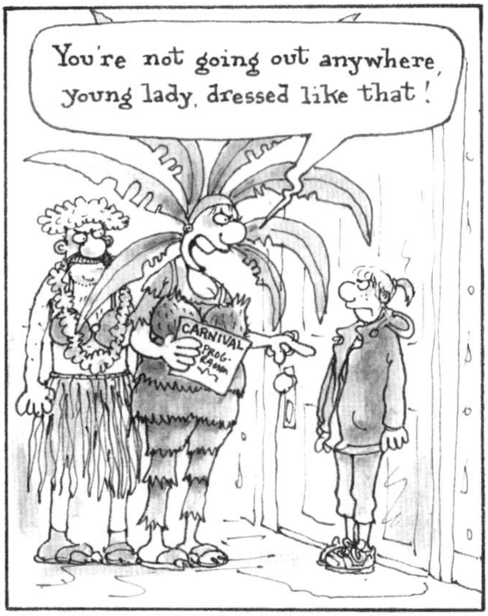
You're not going out anywhere, young lady, dressed like that!
CARNIVAL

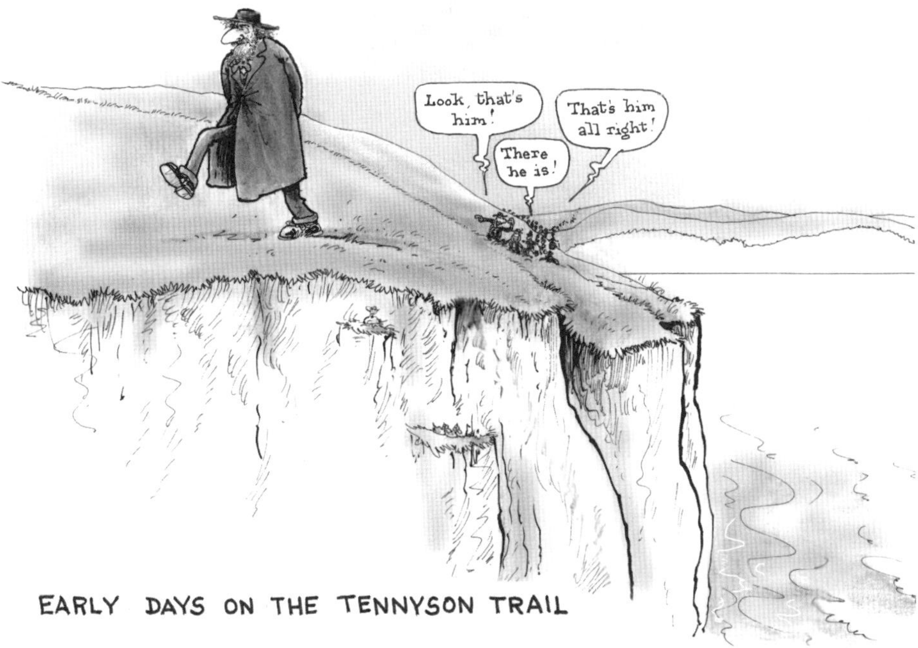
Look, that's him!
There he is!
That's him all right!

EARLY DAYS ON THE TENNYSON TRAIL

NOW THAT THE WALKING FESTIVAL HAS TAKEN OFF SO SUCCESSFULLY, A FEW IDEAS FOR FOLLOW-UPS:

FORKING FESTIVAL?

GAWPING FESTIVAL?

Aw roi? Aw roi! Aw roi- Aw roi Aw roi...

TALKING FESTIVAL?

HOLIDAY SNAPS, 1950s -		
Cowes	Ryde	Carnival
Blackgang	Needles	Ferry

HOLIDAY SNAPS, 2015 -		
Cowes	Ryde	Carnival
Blackgang	Needles	Ferry

..AND A FEW OF THOSE THAT DIDN'T MAKE IT ON TO THE GUEST·LIST FOR THE JUBILEE FLOTILLA:

Ryde Swan

The inevitable annoying jet ski

Past winners of the Cycle Medina Fun Race

Cross·Solent Ferry

SORRY - SAILING CANCELLED FOR OPERATIONAL REASONS

BREAKFAST-TIME AT THE HOTEL STAYED IN BY ENTRANTS TO THE RYDE TOWN·CRIERS COMPETITION:

Good morning!

Christmas Again

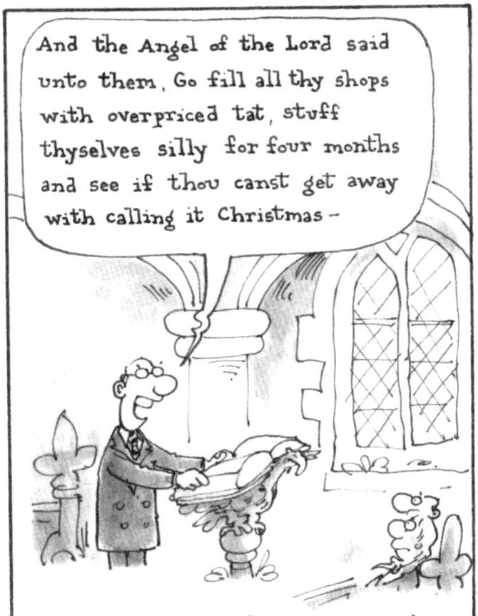
And the Angel of the Lord said unto them, Go fill all thy shops with overpriced tat, stuff thyselves silly for four months and see if thou canst get away with calling it Christmas -

SEASONAL SCRIPTURE (REVISED VERSION)

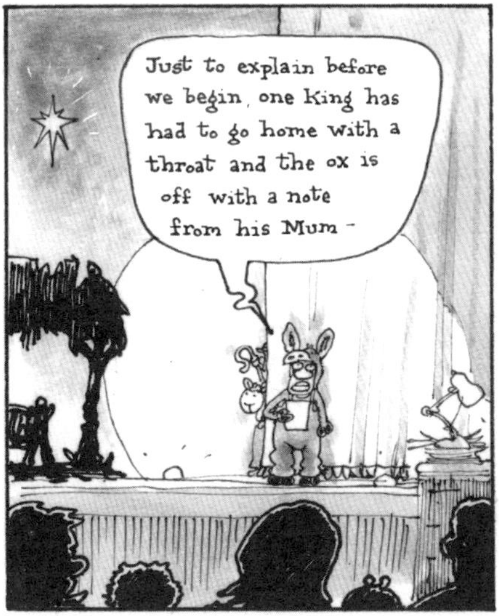
Just to explain before we begin, one King has had to go home with a throat and the ox is off with a note from his Mum -

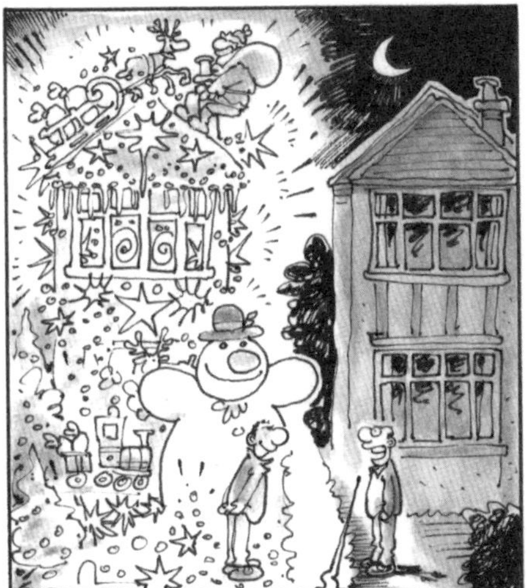

I see you've done your decorations -

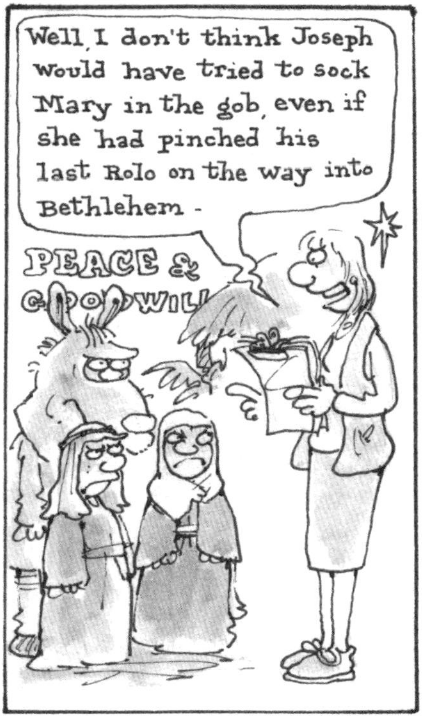
Well, I don't think Joseph would have tried to sock Mary in the gob, even if she had pinched his last Rolo on the way into Bethlehem -
PEACE &

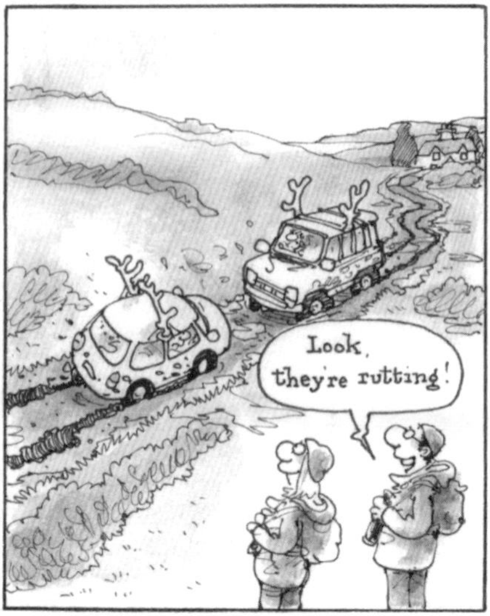
Look, they're rutting!

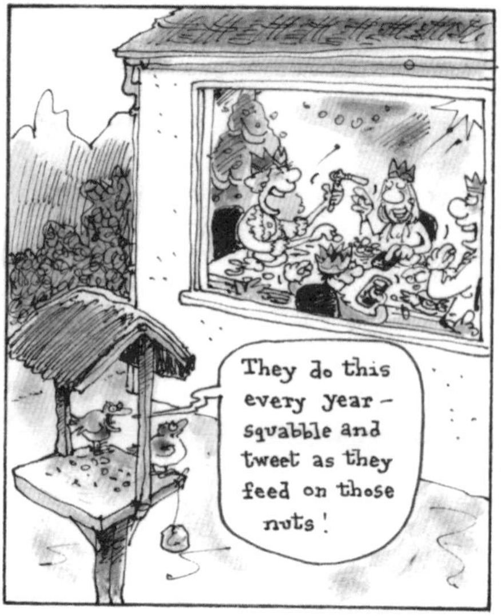
They do this every year - squabble and tweet as they feed on those nuts!

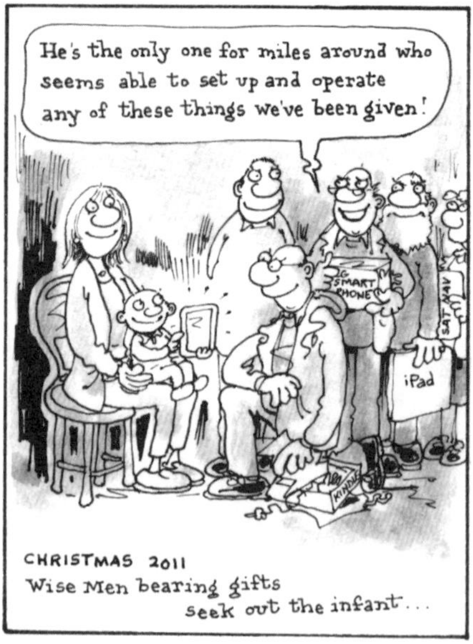
He's the only one for miles around who seems able to set up and operate any of these things we've been given!
SMART PHONE
SAT NAV
iPad
CHRISTMAS 2011
Wise Men bearing gifts seek out the infant...

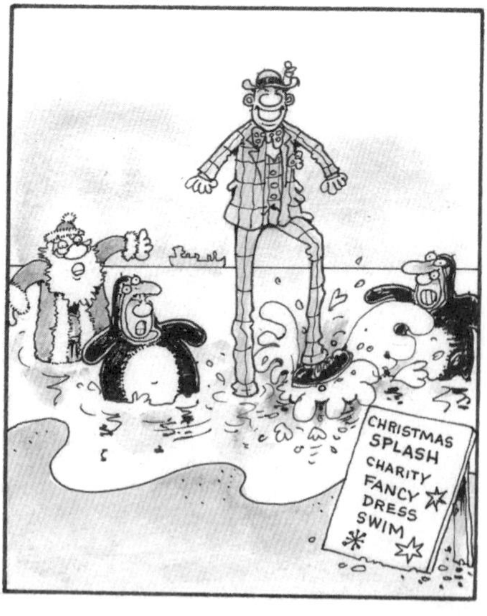
CHRISTMAS SPLASH CHARITY FANCY DRESS SWIM

Season to Taste

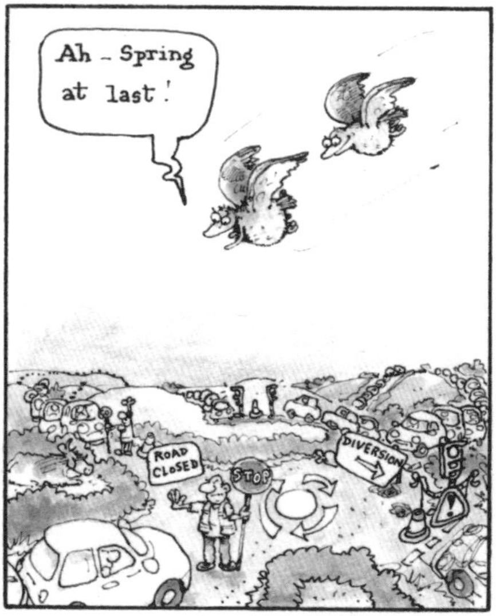
Ah – Spring at last!
ROAD CLOSED
DIVERSION
STOP

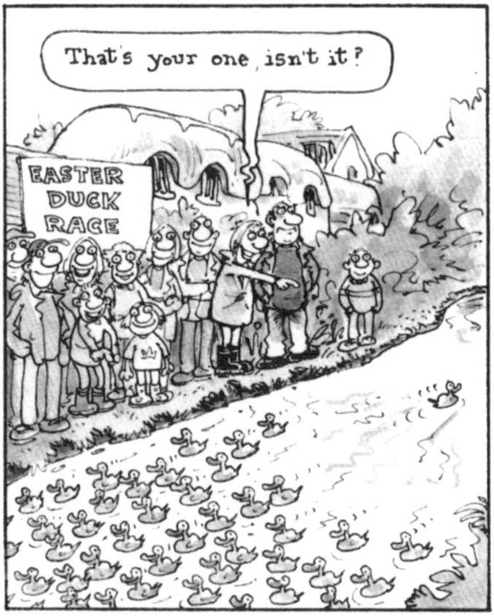
That's your one, isn't it?
EASTER DUCK RACE

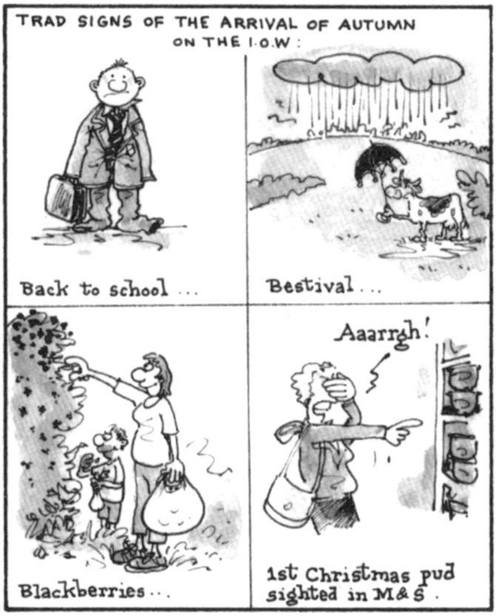
TRAD SIGNS OF THE ARRIVAL OF AUTUMN ON THE I.O.W:
Back to school ...
Bestival ...
Blackberries ...
Aaarrgh!
1st Christmas pud sighted in M&S.

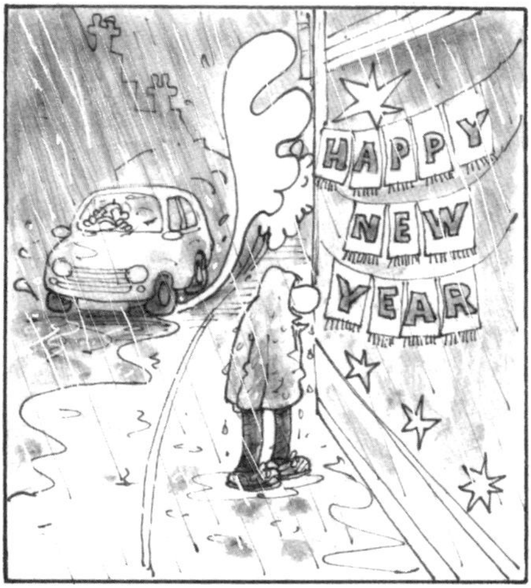
HAPPY NEW YEAR

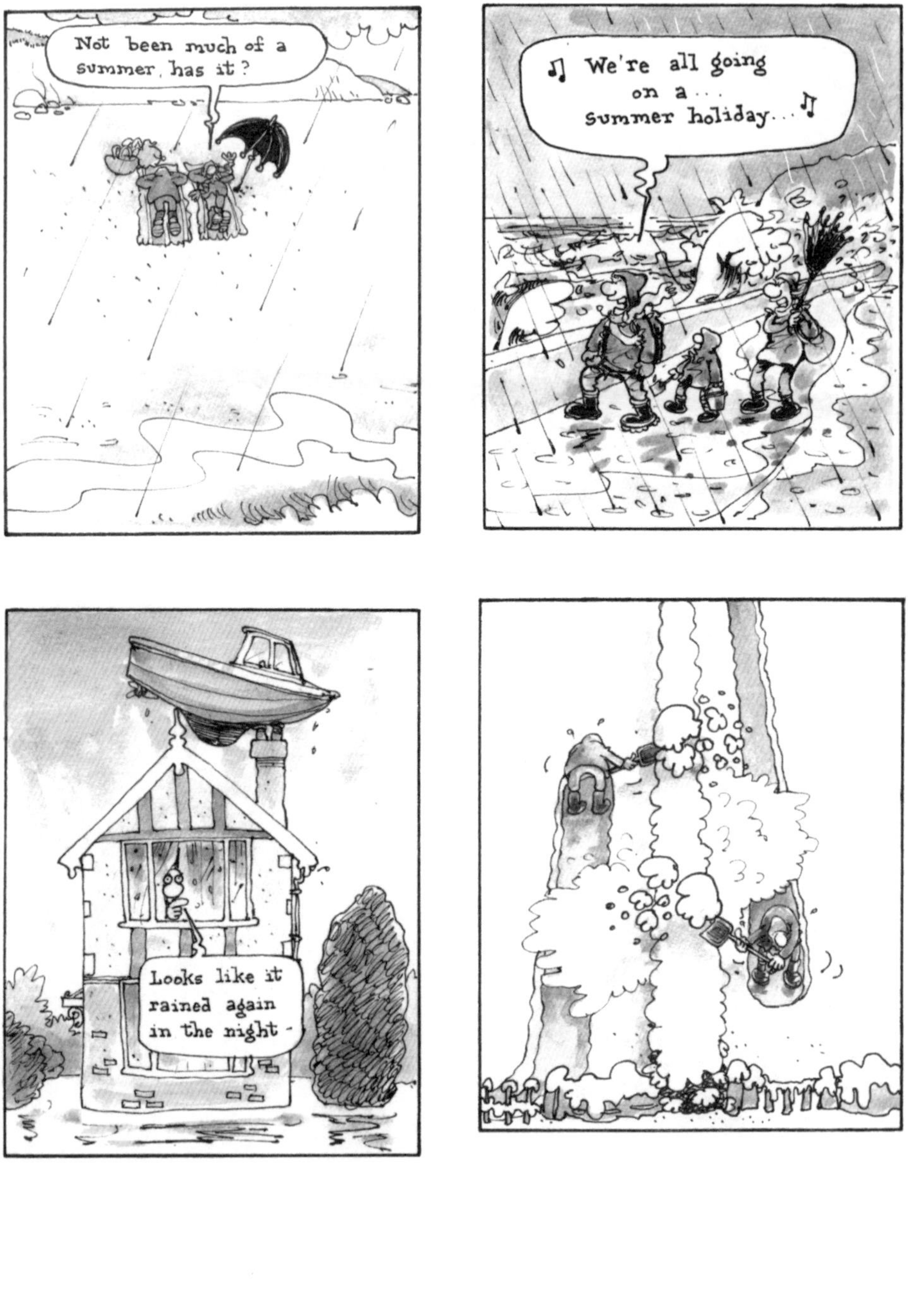
Not been much of a summer, has it?
♫ We're all going on a... summer holiday...♫
Looks like it rained again in the night -

Weather We Like It or Not

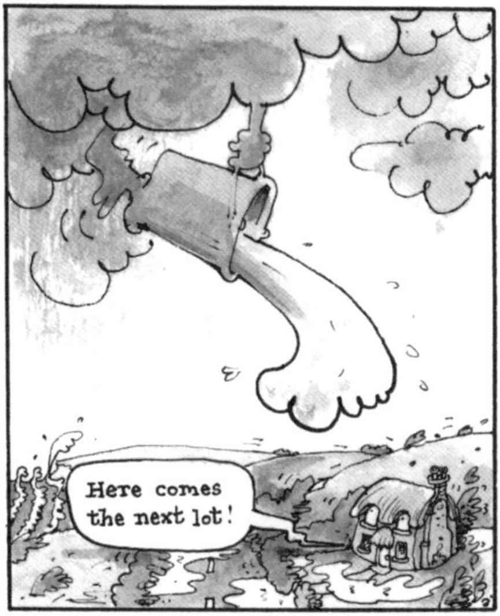
Here comes the next lot!

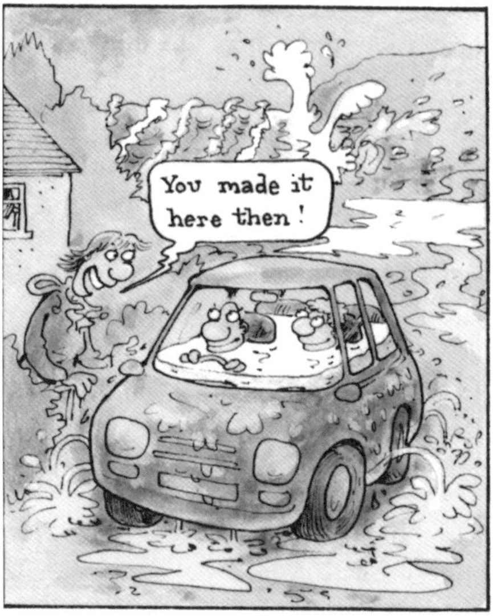
You made it here then!

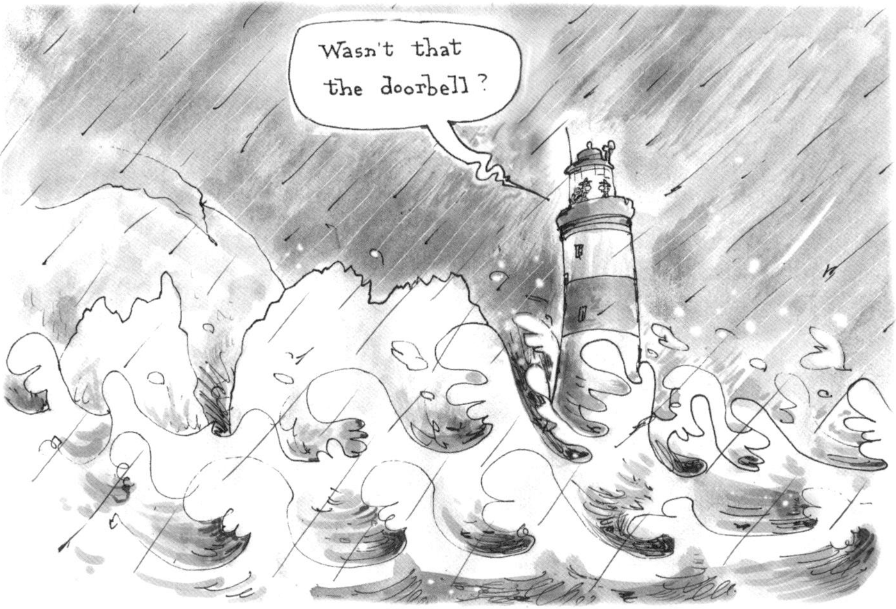
Wasn't that the doorbell?

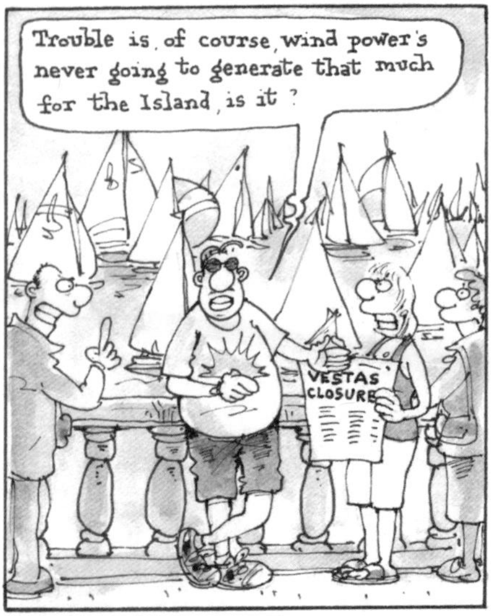
Trouble is, of course, wind power's never going to generate that much for the Island, is it ?
VESTAS CLOSURE

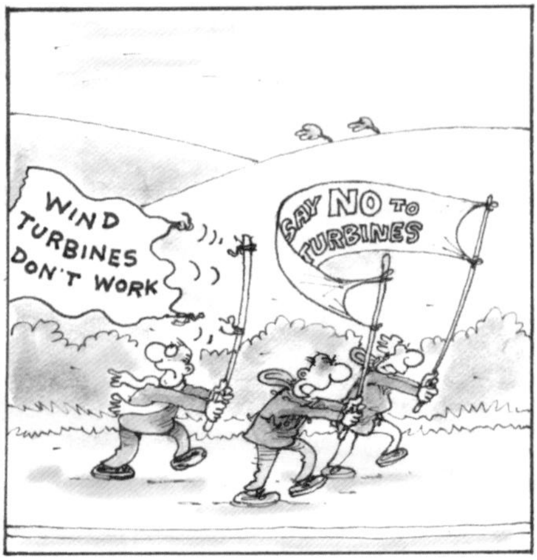
WIND TURBINES DON'T WORK
SAY NO TO TURBINES

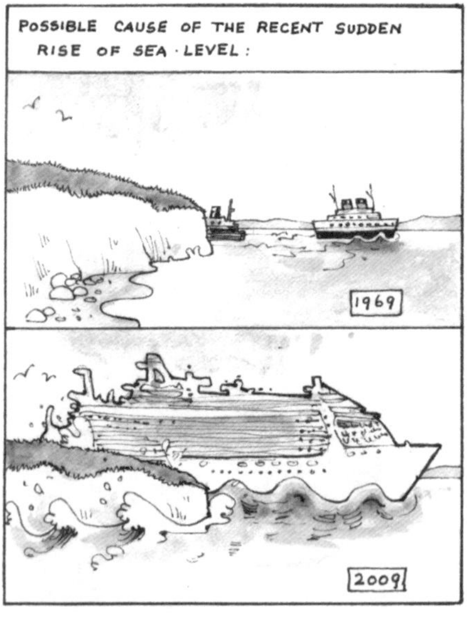
POSSIBLE CAUSE OF THE RECENT SUDDEN RISE OF SEA · LEVEL :
1969
2009

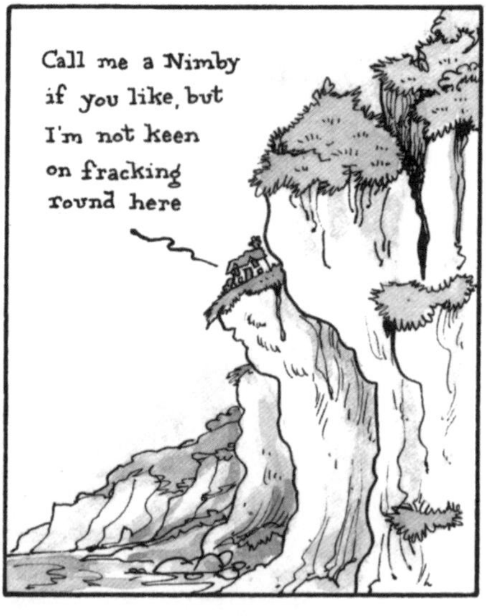
Call me a Nimby if you like, but I'm not keen on fracking round here

Roads & Drivers

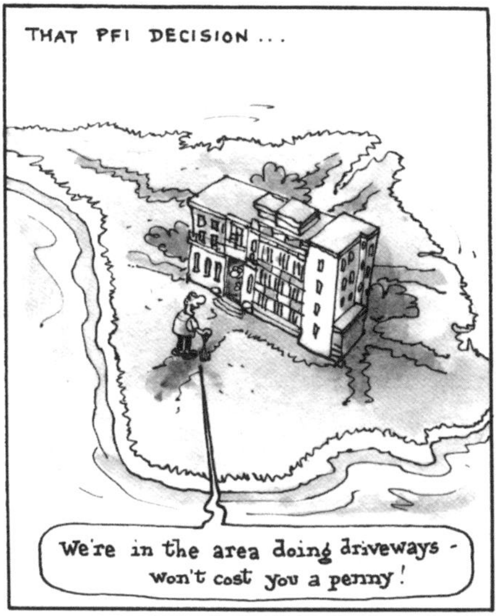
THAT PFI DECISION . . .
We're in the area doing driveways - won't cost you a penny!

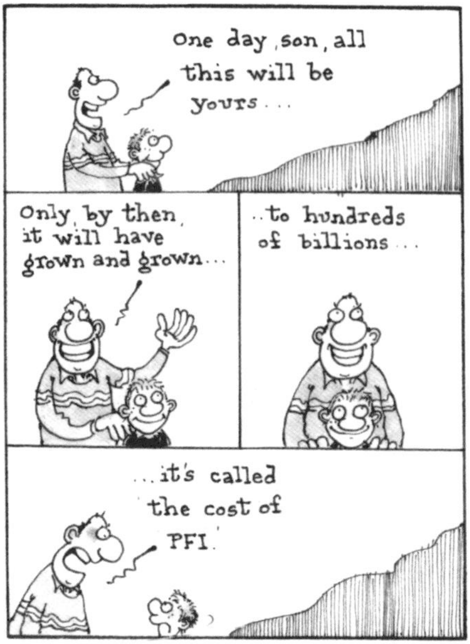
One day, son, all this will be yours . . .
Only, by then, it will have grown and grown . . .
. . to hundreds of billions . . .
. . . it's called the cost of PFI.

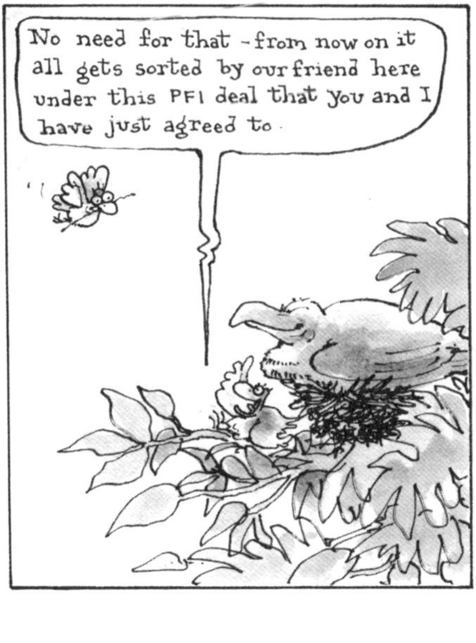
No need for that - from now on it all gets sorted by our friend here under this PFI deal that you and I have just agreed to.

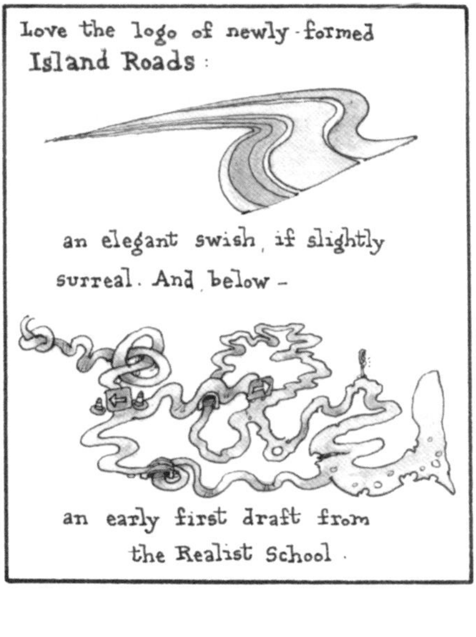
Love the logo of newly-formed Island Roads:
an elegant swish, if slightly surreal. And, below -
an early first draft from the Realist School.

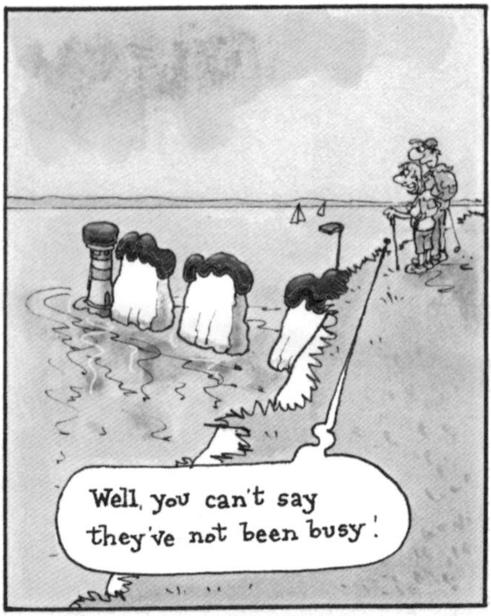
Well, you can't say they've not been busy!

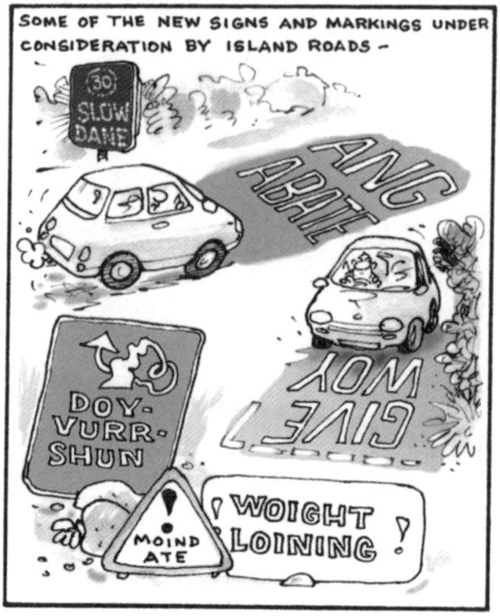
SOME OF THE NEW SIGNS AND MARKINGS UNDER CONSIDERATION BY ISLAND ROADS -
30
SLOW DANE
ANG ABAHT
DOY-VURR-SHUN
GIVE WOY
MOIND ATE
! WOIGHT LOINING !

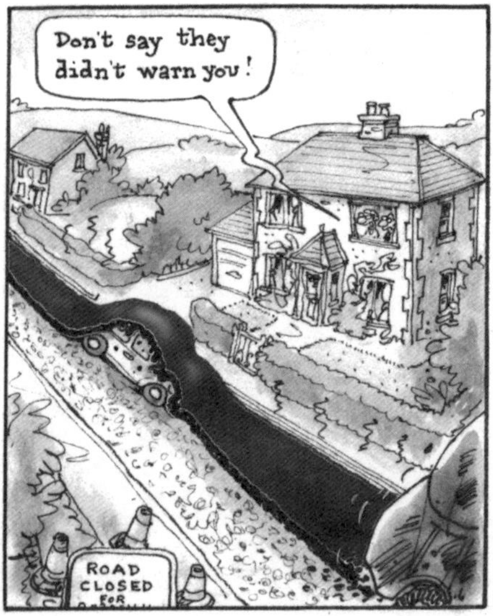
Don't say they didn't warn you!
ROAD CLOSED

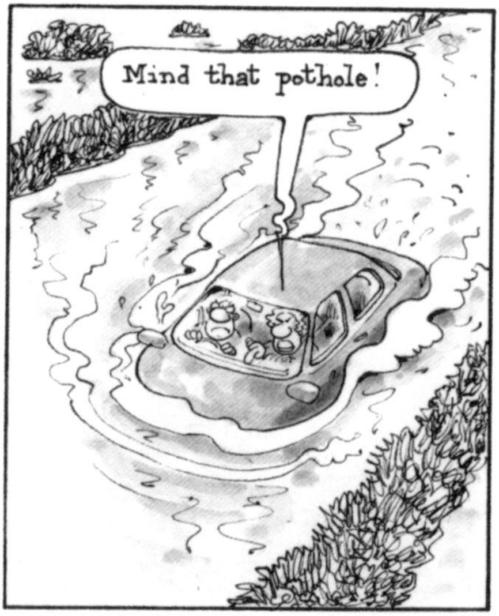
Mind that pothole!

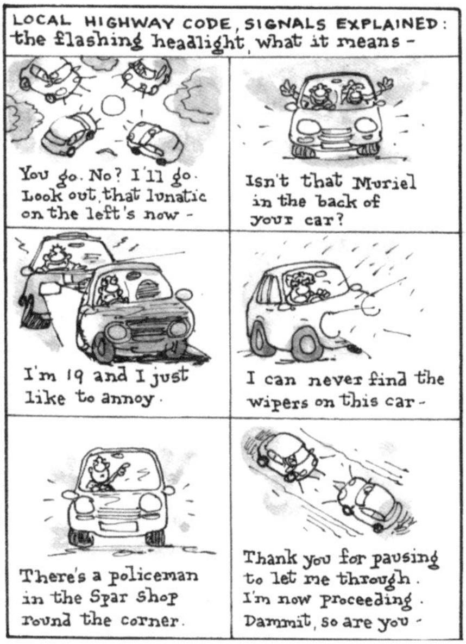
LOCAL HIGHWAY CODE, SIGNALS EXPLAINED: the flashing headlight, what it means -
You go. No? I'll go. Look out, that lunatic on the left's now -
Isn't that Muriel in the back of your car?
I'm 19 and I just like to annoy.
I can never find the wipers on this car -
There's a policeman in the Spar Shop round the corner.
Thank you for pausing to let me through. I'm now proceeding. Dammit, so are you -

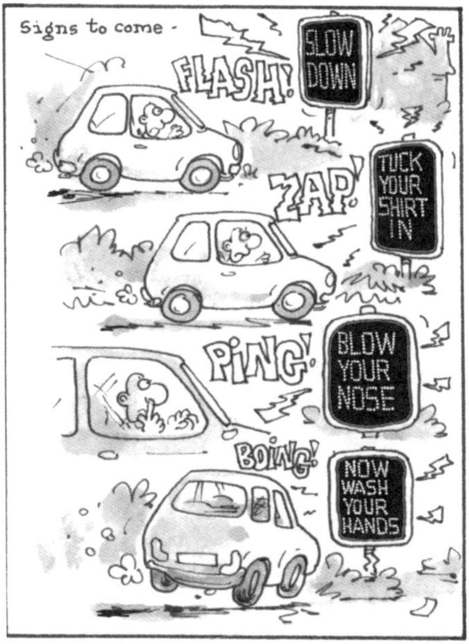
Signs to come -
FLASH!
SLOW DOWN
ZAP!
TUCK YOUR SHIRT IN
PING!
BLOW YOUR NOSE
BOING!
NOW WASH YOUR HANDS

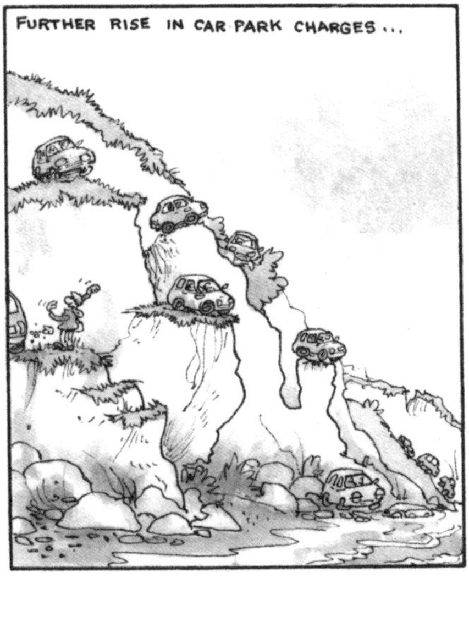
FURTHER RISE IN CAR PARK CHARGES ...

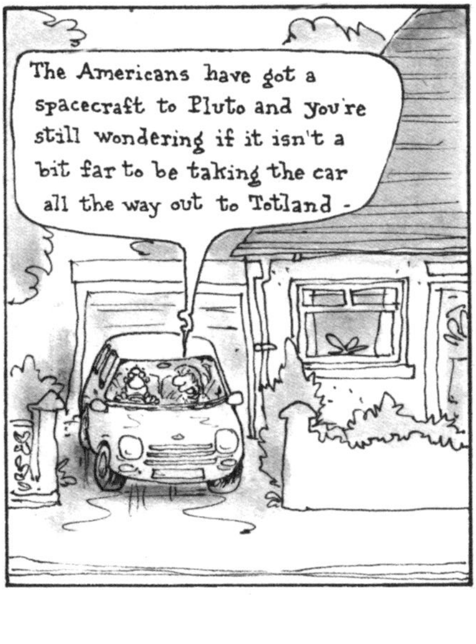
The Americans have got a spacecraft to Pluto and you're still wondering if it isn't a bit far to be taking the car all the way out to Totland -

Freshwater Frolics

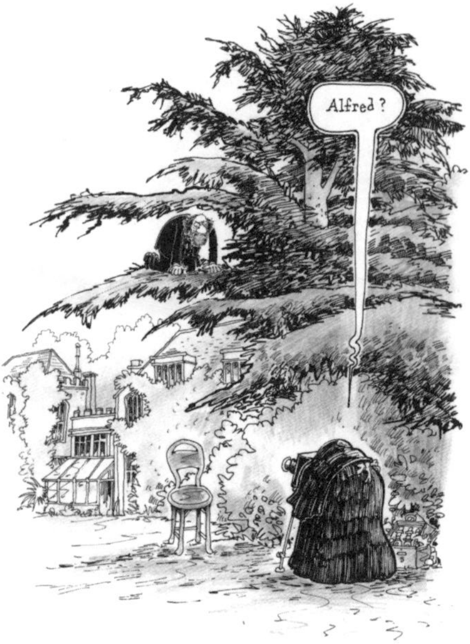
Alfred ?

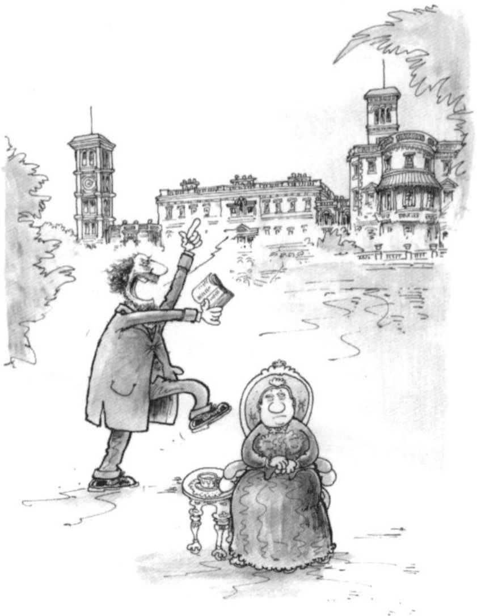

We are not a Muse . . .

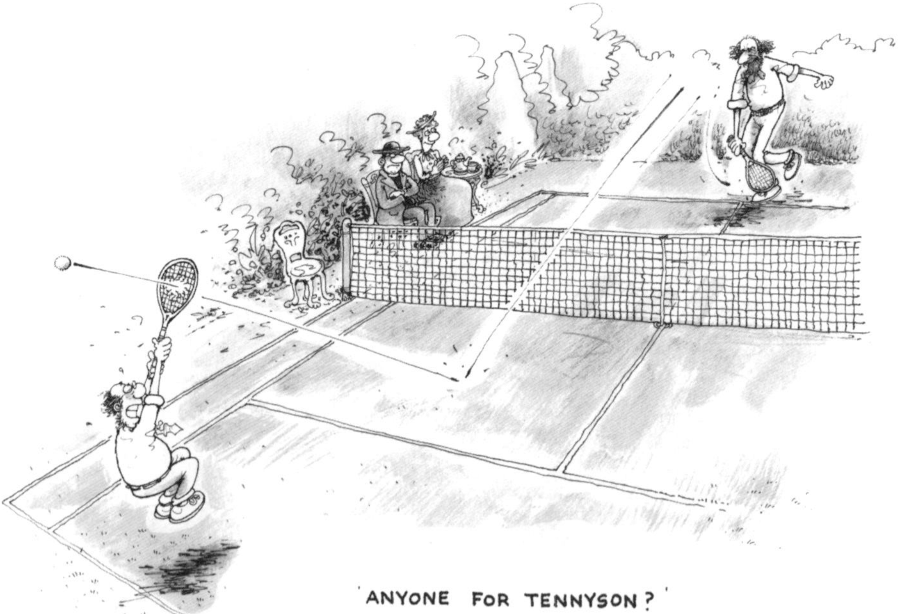

'ANYONE FOR TENNYSON?'

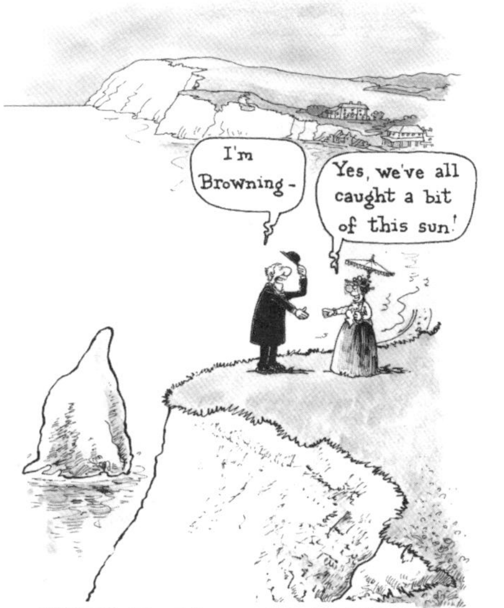
I'm Browning -
Yes, we've all caught a bit of this sun!

FAMOUS VISITORS TO FRESHWATER BAY:
ROBERT BROWNING

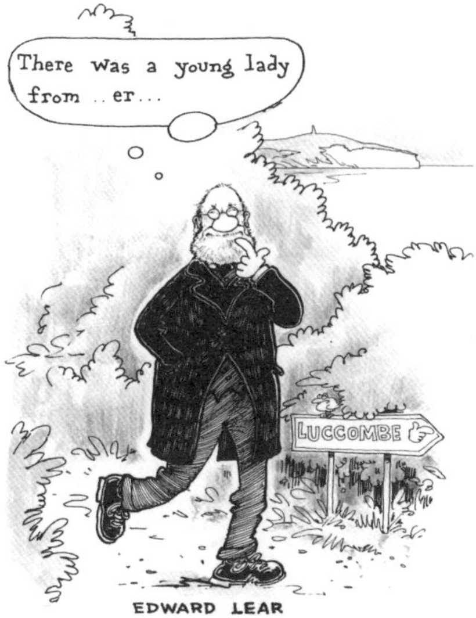
There was a young lady from .. er...
LUCCOMBE

EDWARD LEAR
EXPLORES THE ISLAND

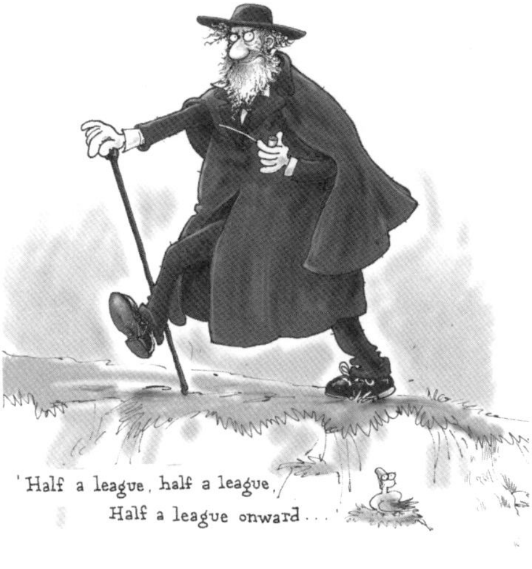
'Half a league, half a league,
Half a league onward...'

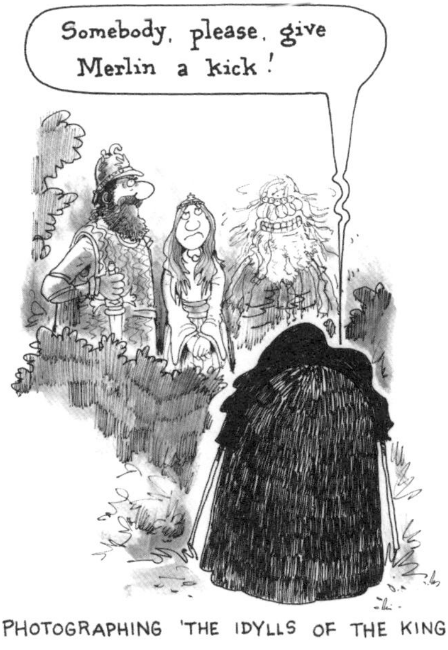
Somebody, please, give Merlin a kick!

PHOTOGRAPHING 'THE IDYLLS OF THE KING'

Around by Bus, by Bike, on Foot

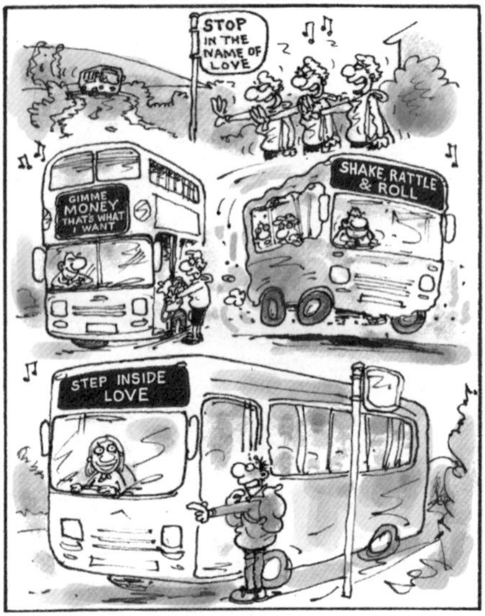
STOP IN THE NAME OF LOVE
GIMME MONEY THAT'S WHAT I WANT
SHAKE, RATTLE & ROLL
STEP INSIDE LOVE

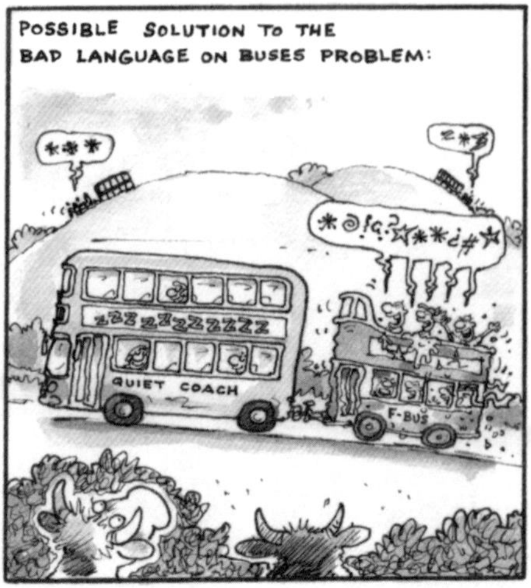
POSSIBLE SOLUTION TO THE BAD LANGUAGE ON BUSES PROBLEM:
QUIET COACH
F-BUS

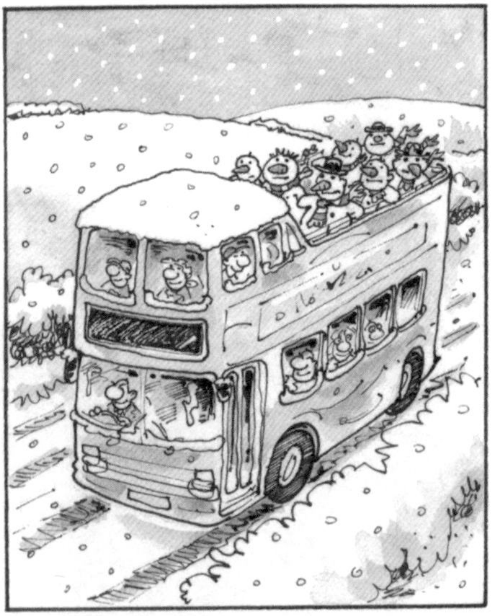

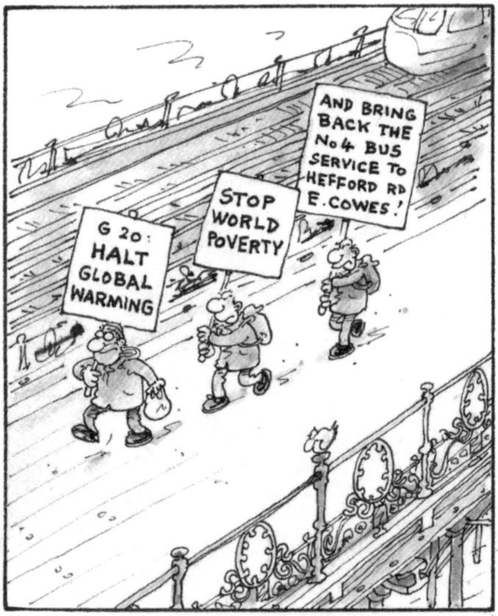
AND BRING BACK THE No 4 BUS SERVICE TO HEFFORD RD E. COWES!
STOP WORLD POVERTY
G 20: HALT GLOBAL WARMING

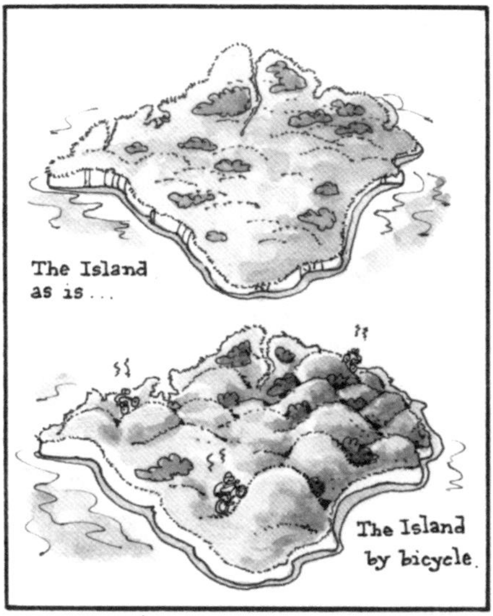
The Island as is...
The Island by bicycle.

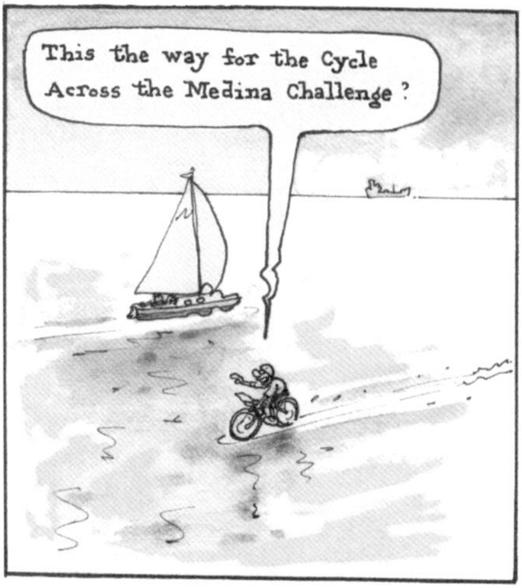
This the way for the Cycle Across the Medina Challenge?

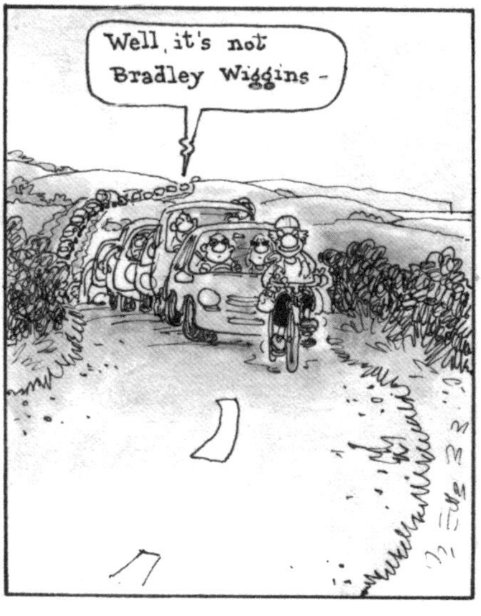
Well, it's not Bradley Wiggins -

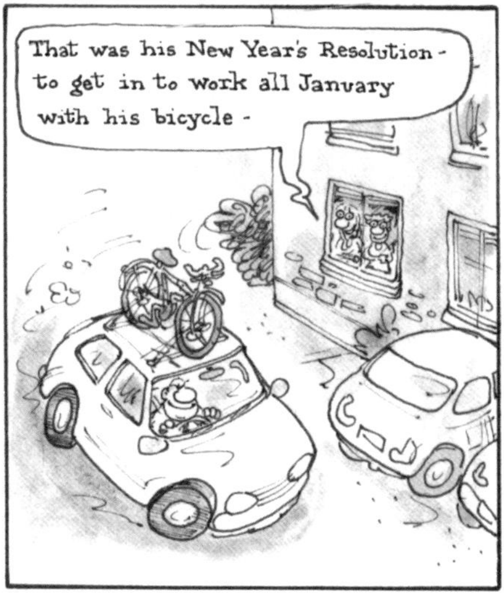
That was his New Year's Resolution - to get in to work all January with his bicycle -

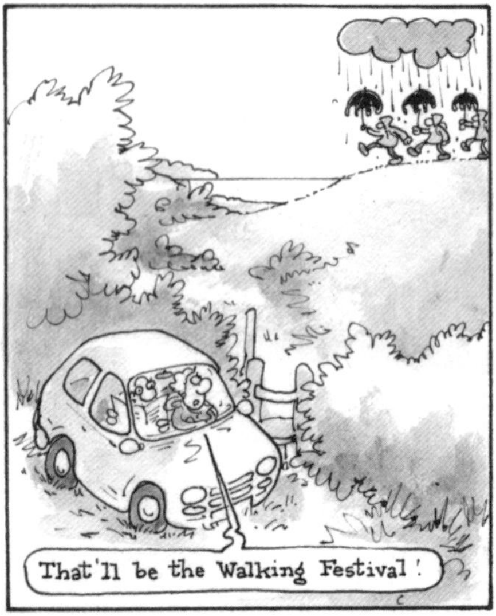
That'll be the Walking Festival!

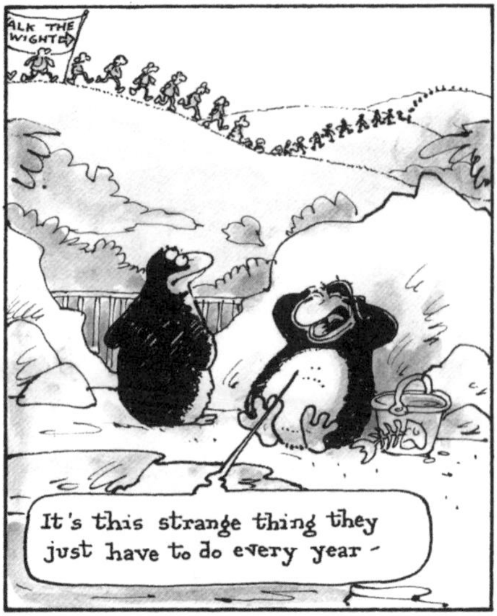
ALK THE WIGHT
It's this strange thing they just have to do every year -

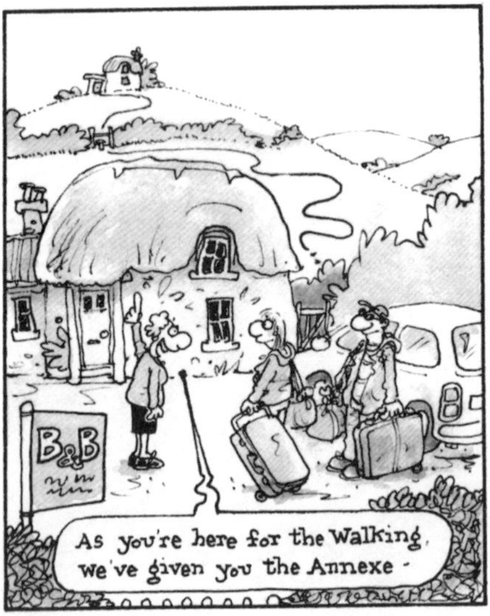
B&B
As you're here for the Walking, we've given you the Annexe -

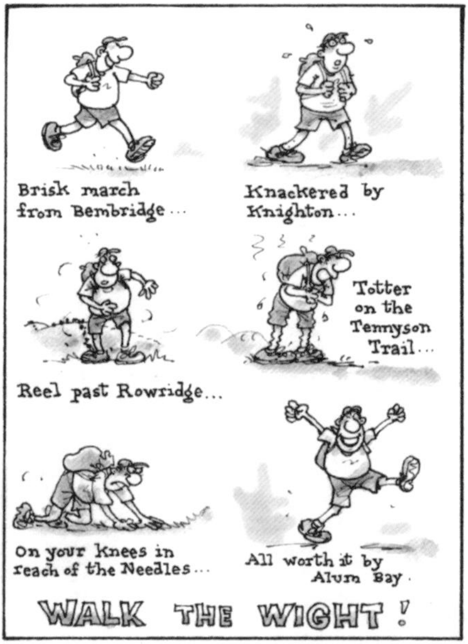
Brisk march from Bembridge...
Knackered by Knighton...
Reel past Rowridge...
Totter on the Tennyson Trail...
On your knees in reach of the Needles...
All worth it by Alum Bay.
WALK THE WIGHT!

Sport on Land & Sea

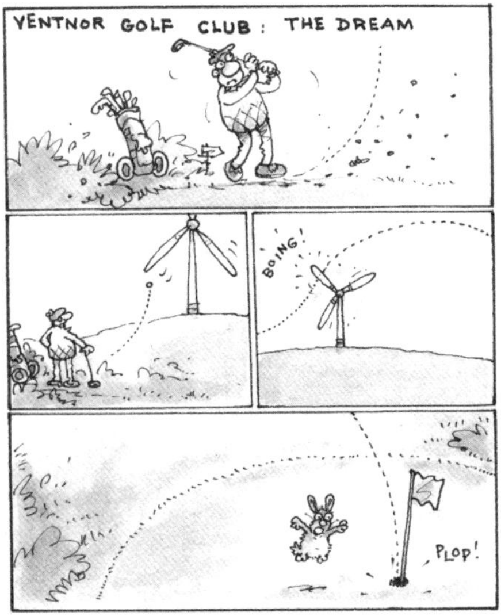
VENTNOR GOLF CLUB : THE DREAM
BOING!
PLOP!

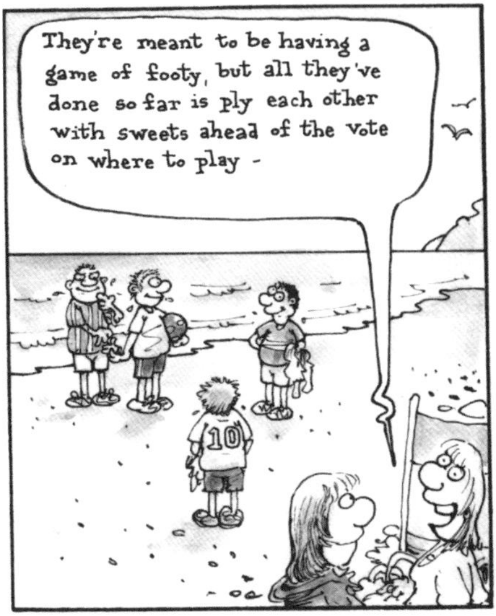
They're meant to be having a game of footy, but all they've done so far is ply each other with sweets ahead of the vote on where to play -

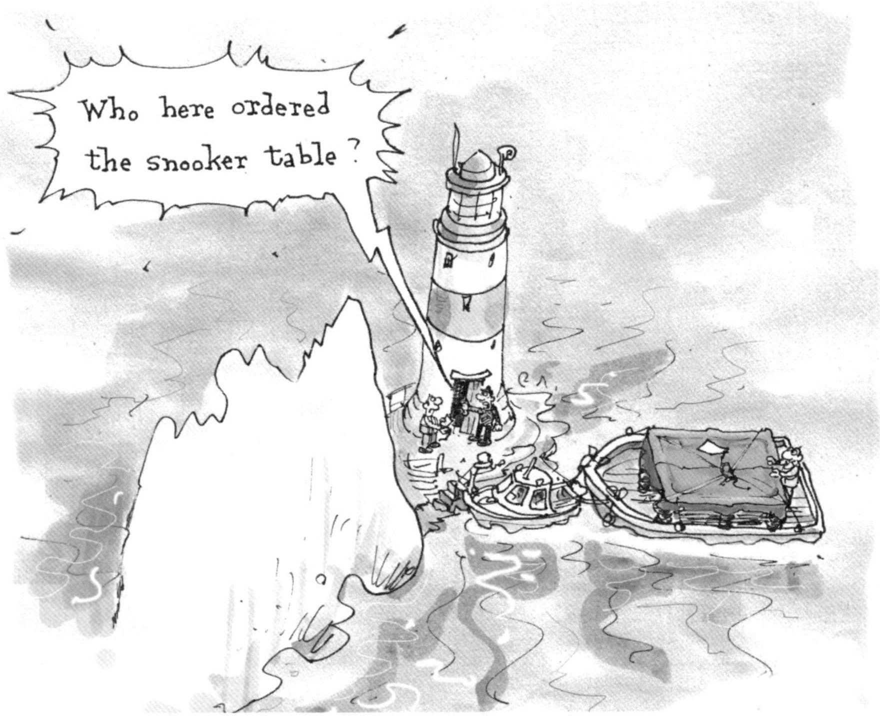
Who here ordered the snooker table?

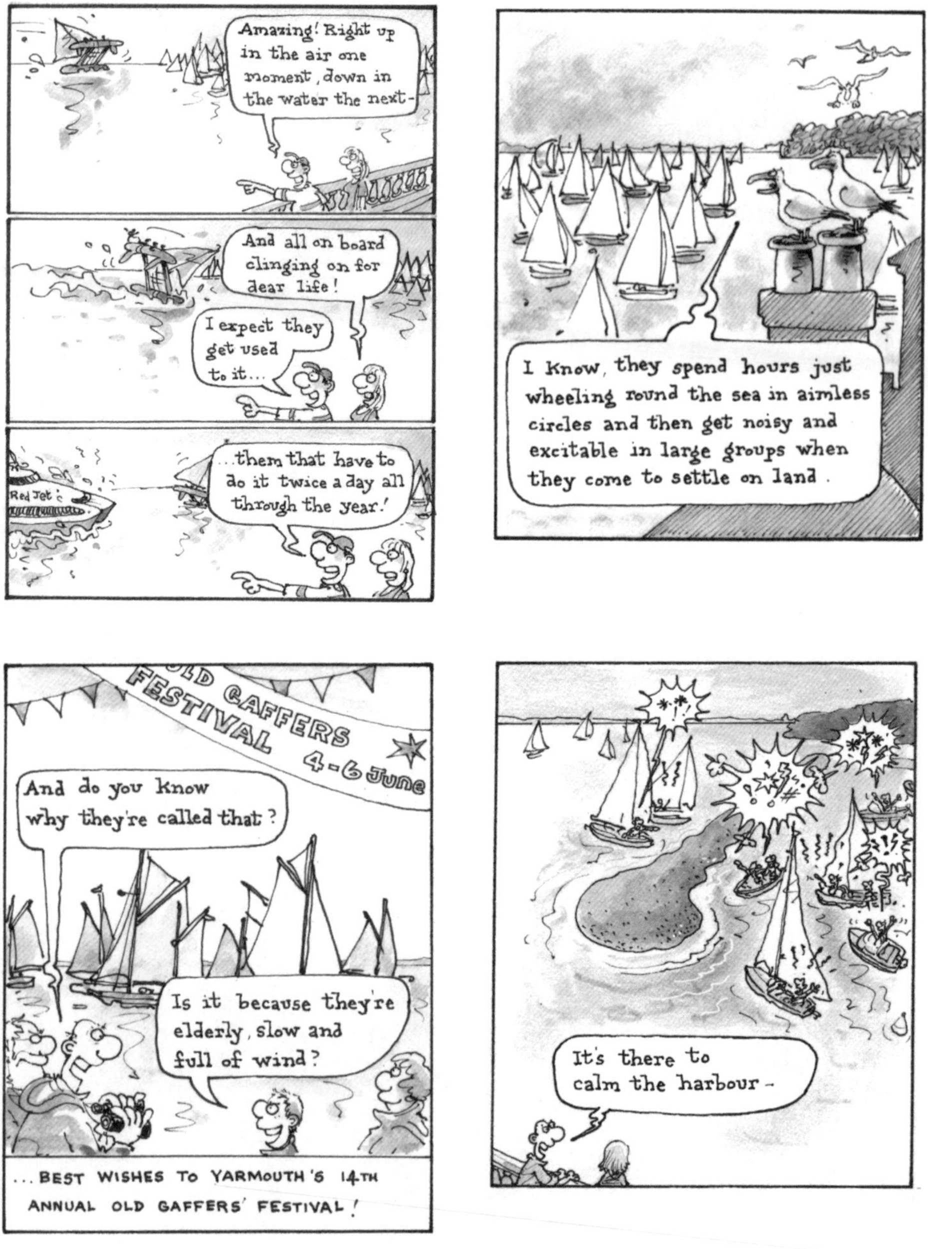

Amazing! Right up in the air one moment, down in the water the next-
And all on board clinging on for dear life!
I expect they get used to it...
Red Jet
...them that have to do it twice a day all through the year!
I know, they spend hours just wheeling round the sea in aimless circles and then get noisy and excitable in large groups when they come to settle on land.
LD GAFFERS FESTIVAL 4-6 June
And do you know why they're called that?
Is it because they're elderly, slow and full of wind?
...BEST WISHES TO YARMOUTH'S 14TH ANNUAL OLD GAFFERS' FESTIVAL!
It's there to calm the harbour-

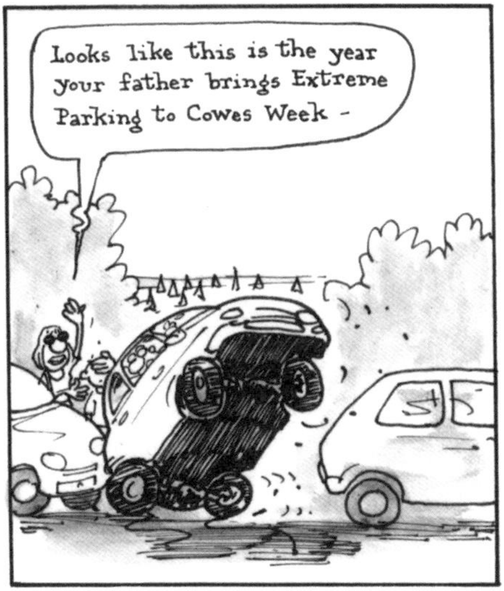
Looks like this is the year your father brings Extreme Parking to Cowes Week -

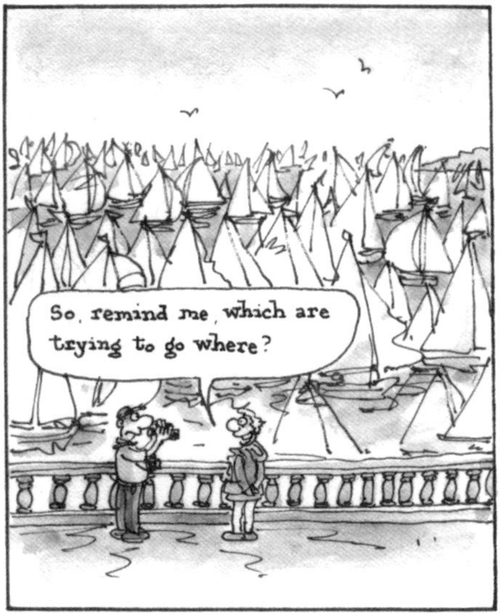
So, remind me, which are trying to go where?

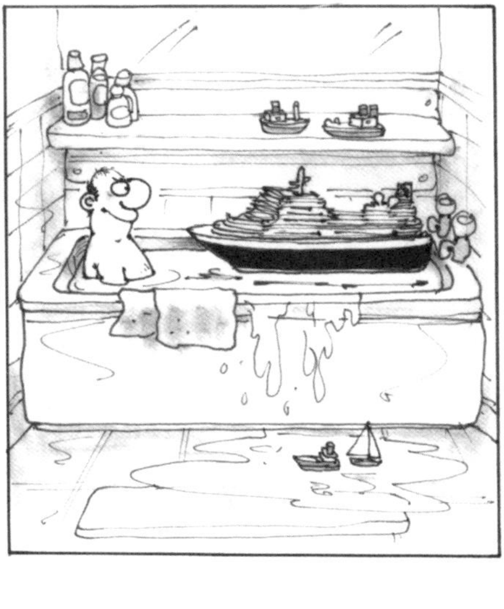

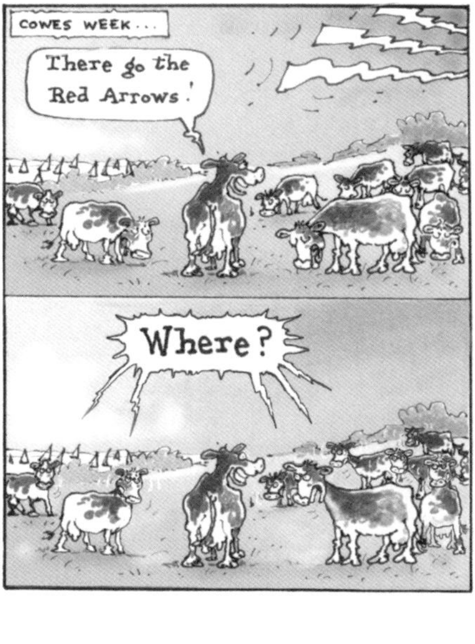
COWES WEEK...
There go the Red Arrows!
Where?

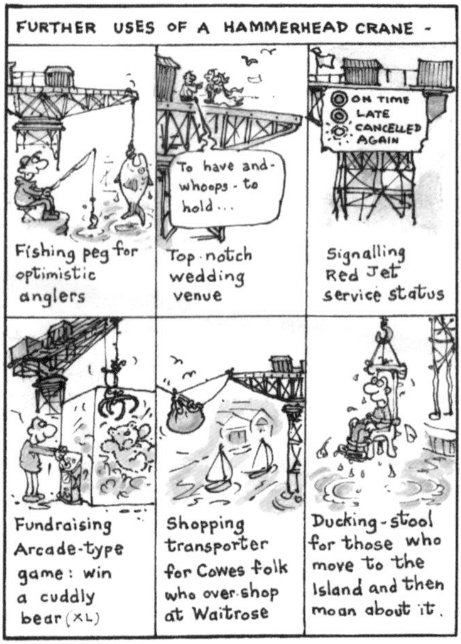
FURTHER USES OF A HAMMERHEAD CRANE -
Fishing peg for optimistic anglers
To have and - whoops - to hold ...
Top-notch wedding venue
ON TIME
LATE
CANCELLED
AGAIN
Signalling Red Jet service status
Fundraising Arcade-type game: win a cuddly bear (XL)
Shopping transporter for Cowes folk who over-shop at Waitrose
Ducking-stool for those who move to the Island and then moan about it.

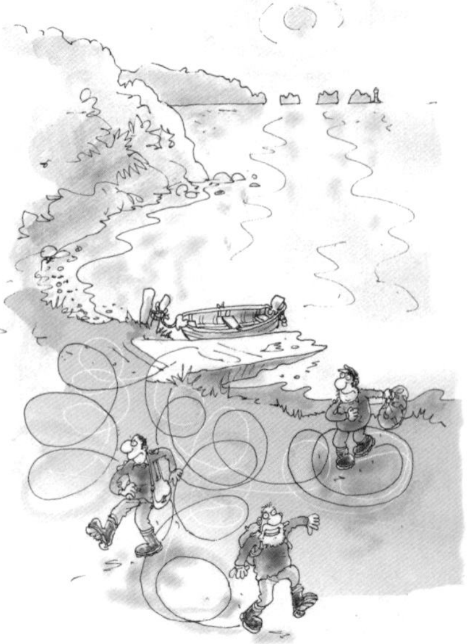

Lost fragments of local history:

KEEPERS FROM THE NEEDLES LIGHTHOUSE
STEP ASHORE AT THE END OF A 3-MONTH TOUR OF DUTY.

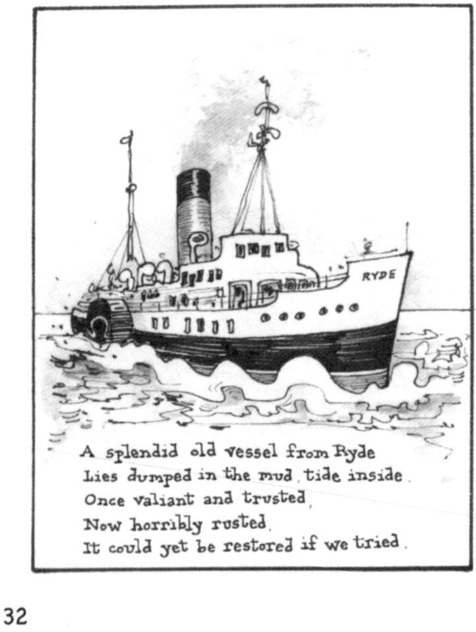
RYDE

A splendid old vessel from Ryde
Lies dumped in the mud, tide inside.
Once valiant and trusted,
Now horribly rusted,
It could yet be restored if we tried.

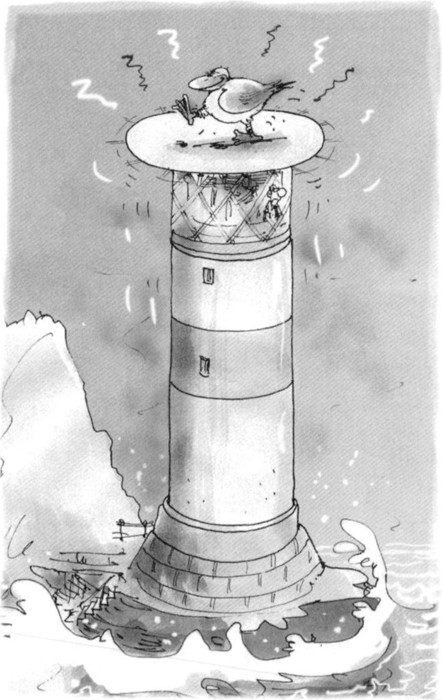

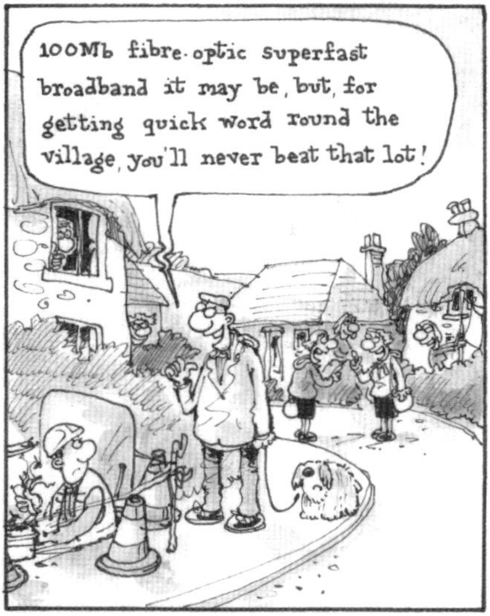
100Mb fibre-optic superfast broadband it may be, but, for getting quick word round the village, you'll never beat that lot!

THIS CARTOON HAS HAD DIGITAL SWITCHOVER

[- try banging it
- or, to get our friendly engineer to call, try our busy switchboard on Mumbai 0413 282828282828]

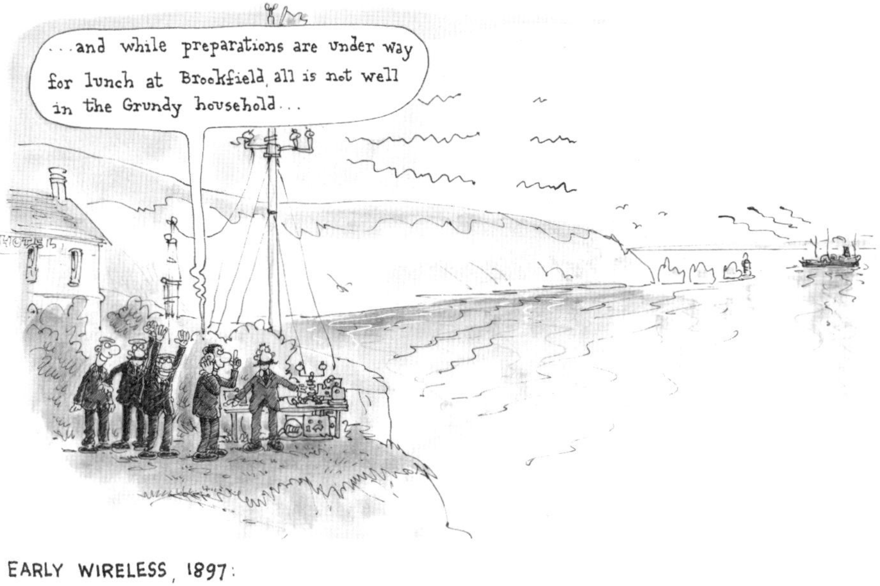
...and while preparations are under way for lunch at Brookfield, all is not well in the Grundy household...

EARLY WIRELESS, 1897:
MARCONI SUCCEEDS IN RECEIVING WIRELESS SIGNALS ACROSS THE WAVES IN ALUM BAY

THE Island

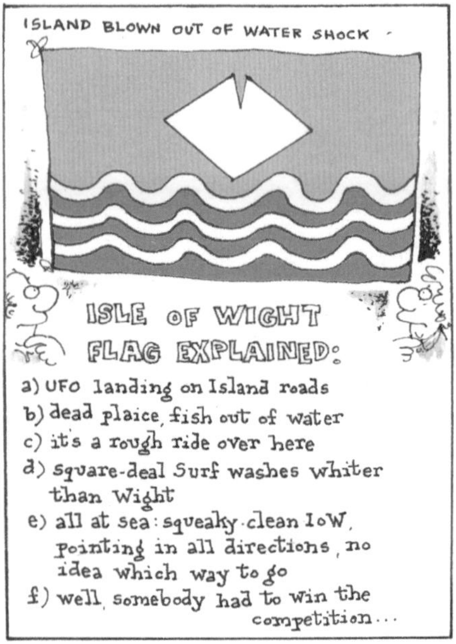
ISLAND BLOWN OUT OF WATER SHOCK
ISLE OF WIGHT FLAG EXPLAINED:
a) UFO landing on Island roads
b) dead plaice, fish out of water
c) it's a rough ride over here
d) square-deal Surf washes whiter than Wight
e) all at sea: squeaky-clean IoW, pointing in all directions, no idea which way to go
f) well, somebody had to win the competition...

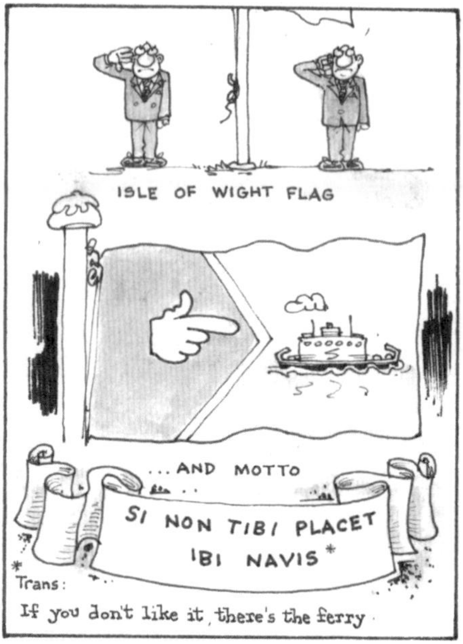
ISLE OF WIGHT FLAG
...AND MOTTO
SI NON TIBI PLACET IBI NAVIS *
* Trans:
If you don't like it, there's the ferry.

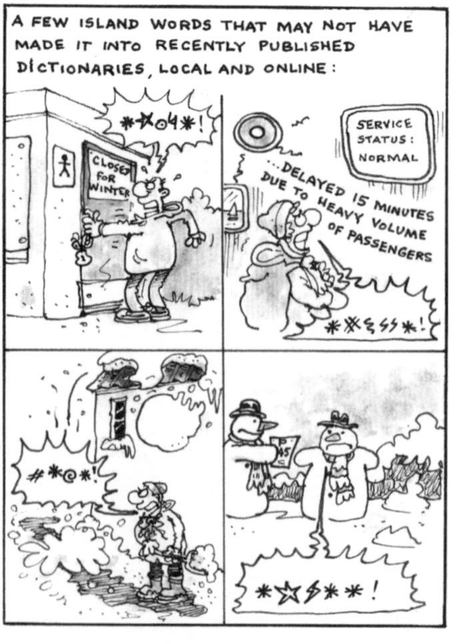
A FEW ISLAND WORDS THAT MAY NOT HAVE MADE IT INTO RECENTLY PUBLISHED DICTIONARIES, LOCAL AND ONLINE:
CLOSED FOR WINTER
SERVICE STATUS: NORMAL
...DELAYED 15 MINUTES DUE TO HEAVY VOLUME OF PASSENGERS

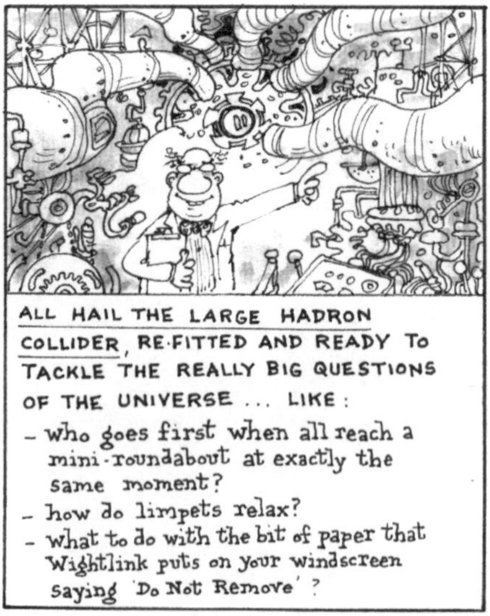
ALL HAIL THE LARGE HADRON COLLIDER, RE-FITTED AND READY TO TACKLE THE REALLY BIG QUESTIONS OF THE UNIVERSE ... LIKE:
- who goes first when all reach a mini-roundabout at exactly the same moment?
- how do limpets relax?
- what to do with the bit of paper that Wightlink puts on your windscreen saying 'Do Not Remove'?

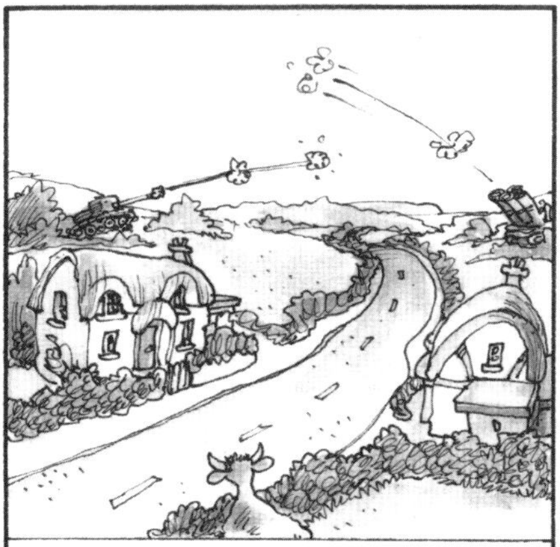

Aug 2013 – and first shots are fired in the civil war breaking out between those who call it IW and those who insist it's IOW.

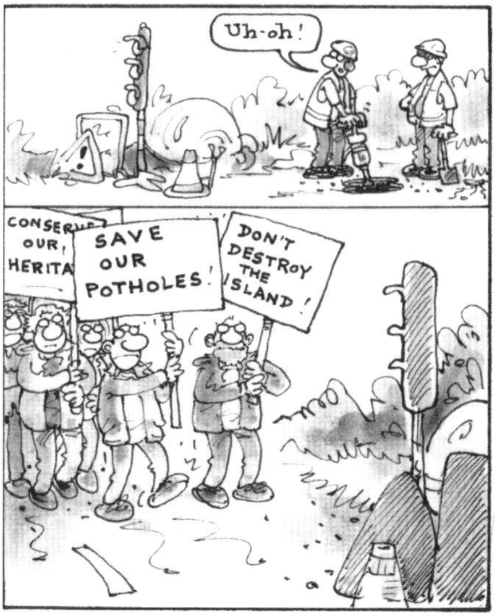
Uh-oh!
CONSERVE OUR HERITA
SAVE OUR POTHOLES!
DON'T DESTROY THE ISLAND!

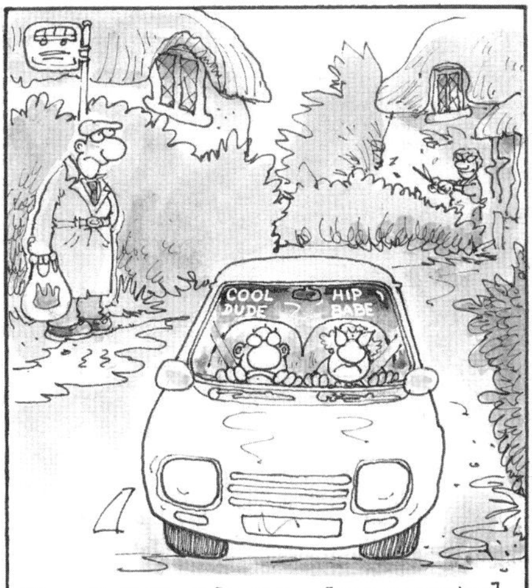
COOL DUDE
HIP BABE

Now that the Island has been recognised as 'cool' (Harper's Bazaar) and 'appealing to a new, hip crowd' (or maybe 'new-hip crowd'?)...

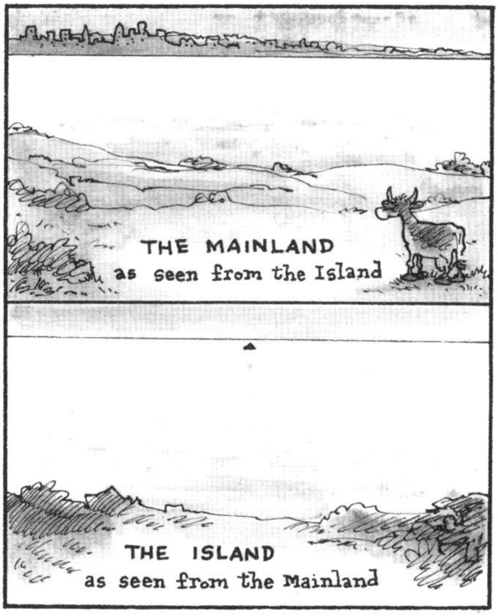
THE MAINLAND
as seen from the Island
THE ISLAND
as seen from the Mainland

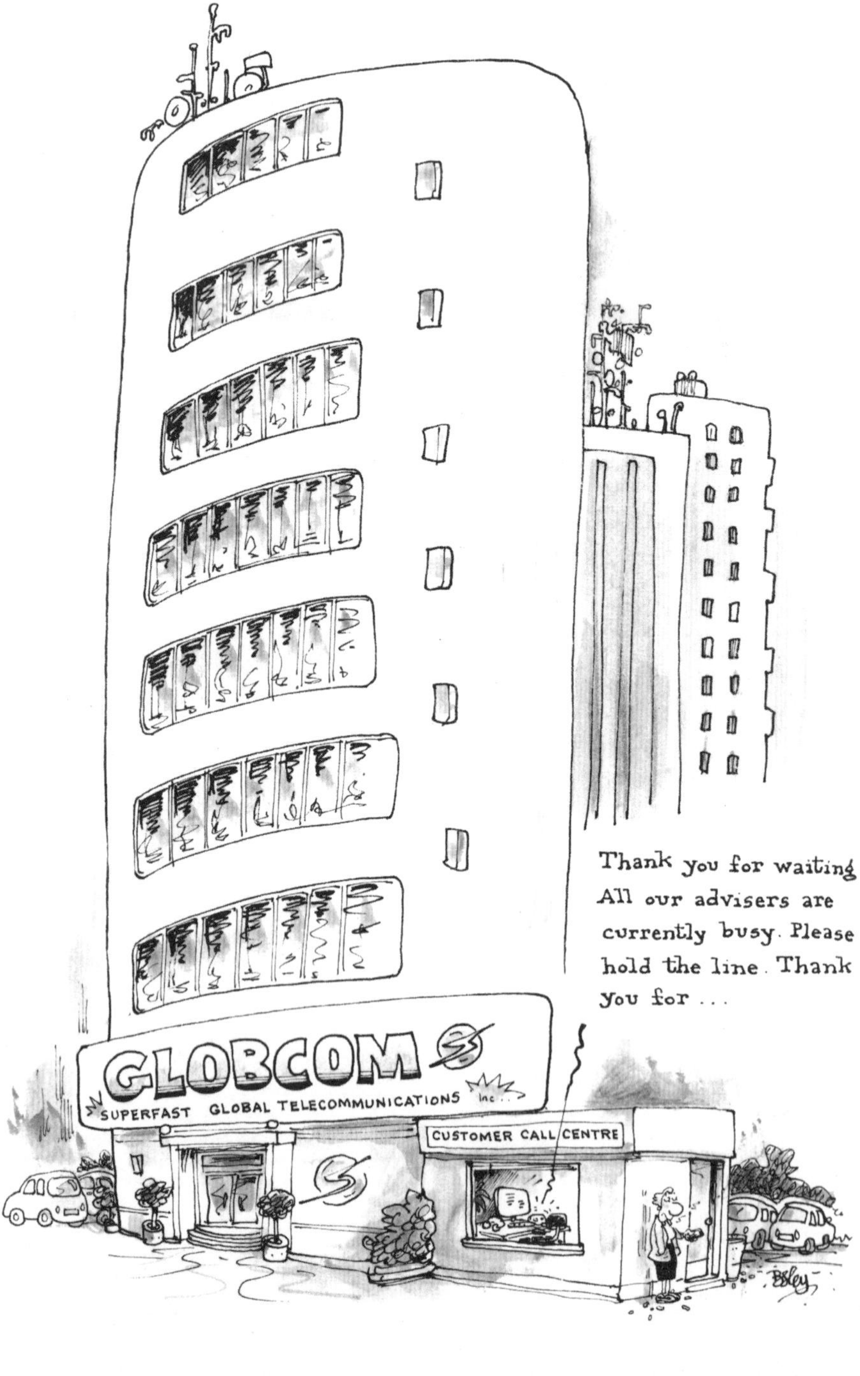
Thank you for waiting. All our advisers are currently busy. Please hold the line. Thank you for ...
GLOBCOM
SUPERFAST GLOBAL TELECOMMUNICATIONS Inc.
CUSTOMER CALL CENTRE
Bisley